The Peacocking Man

RICHARD JOHNSON

Copyright © 2023 Richard Johnson

All rights reserved.

ISBN: 9798388083791

DEDICATION

To my mum, words cannot describe my love for you.

CONTENTS

	Prologue	1-2
1	Pander	3-11
2	Nonsense	12-19
3	Responsibility	20-33
4	Communication	34-42
5	His best friend	43-56
6	Jealousy	57-64
7	Cheating	65-79
8	Breaking up	80-88
9	Sex	89-101
10	Narcissism	102-111
11	LBJ	112-121

ABOUT THE AUTHOR

Richard is an expert on Narcissistic Personality Disorder and a long-time campaigner for women and minority rights.

For 10 years he was CEO of one of the top book publishers in the UK and the industry's most controversial boss, its disruptor in chief.

He grew Bonnier Publishing's sales from $10m to $150m, publishing books by many of the top stars including Robbie Williams, Roger Daltery, Burt Reynolds, Lilly Allen and Gary Barlow. He was the driving force behind the rise of the *Youtuber* book publishing craze and created the biggest signing in UK publishing history when a crowd of 8,000 teenagers descended on central London to get a chance to meet Alfie Deyes, the author of *"The Pointless Book"*.

He also brought into the UK the *"Tattooist of Auschwitz"*, which was the biggest selling book in the UK over the years 2018 and 2019.

During his time with Bonnier Publishing, he was the industry's champion of women rights, BAME rights and the employment of non-university educated men and women into an industry which was and still remains very conservative and traditional.

By the time he left, every one of his group Division Heads (UK, Australia, USA) was a woman, his deputy was a woman, 76% of the 500 people working for him were women, his head of HR was a woman, his head of PR was a woman and all of the highest paid people in the group, apart from him were women. Two of the three division heads were BAME (Black Asian Minority Ethnic) the only publishing group in the whole of the UK to have such a profile. Richard had appointed them all. One of them, Perminder Mann, who was his replacement at Bonnier, is now constantly on TV debating BAME issues. He had initially appointed her into his sales team and then over a 5-year period rapidly promoted her to be his deputy.

He is a now a best-selling author in his own right, with his book "Show Me Your Medals"

"This is a book about heterosexual man. It tells the secrets of mankind in quite often a light hearted and stereotypical way. I appreciate fully I often generalise and not everything I write applies to every single man, that would be impossible, but certain aspects of what I say definitely does.

Especially the sex parts.

We are all basic like that as you will discover on this journey.

This isn't a book about me, it's a story compiled from hours of research, interviews, surveys and my observations of mankind over many years.

This book is for ladies essentially but men should read it too because what it reveals is a wakeup call for mankind, on top of all the other wake up calls they have had over the centuries.

In this book, I make jokes about men and society a lot. Often tongue in cheek and with huge amounts of irony. This doesn't undermine the seriousness of the points I make it simply makes it an easier read. Humour highlights mankind's stupidity it doesn't justify it. And where I can, I tell some stories to showcase my own stupidity.

I say things in this book other commentators are probably too scared too. and as such the language is sometimes from the "street," because, well, most of us are. I highlight what men think, I don't condone it in fact as I wrote more and more I became increasing more and more ashamed of mankind.

As you will soon discover."

Richard Johnson March 2023
www.thelionheart.co.uk

PROLOGUE

I love you.

Those 3 words, if meant, if truly meant, change everything.

Real love.

It is a feeling of inner spiritually which can't ever be explained or described because it is so toxically mesmerising. It's a volcanic supernova inside of you, so strong, so powerful, it even transcends that of Romeo and Juliet.

It's the emotion which allows you to breath at last, the oxygen of Gods, and you are now the chosen one. It's the dream of all eternity, the dream of your one life, the dream that no one else can ever understand if they don't experience it. It's the dream that Prince Charming will arrive to swoop you up and protect you forever no matter what battles lay ahead in your life.

For richer, for poorer in sickness and in health. Real love though, not a throwaway comment in a text message.

The love that petrifies you at the very thought of losing it. It's a love that you desperately want to believe in, so much so you may even have to run from it. It's an emotion that walks on a slim tightrope between the evilest hatred and the most wonderous heaven. It is passionate, exhilarating, it is so powerful in its wonderous silence that it won't ever leave you even in the darkest of moments.

But it's the worst kind of addiction because you know injecting it into your soul will give you the most incredible high but you are equally aware that the come down from not having it will be just too painful to bear.

It's the three words of cupid's impossible promise. You are terrified to hear them spoken, yet you still crave it to be shouted from every rooftop, because you know it's the feeling that you will never again have if you lose the love of your life.

You catch what you think is the wave of love at the start of a relationship, but that is sometimes a love of fool's hope, it is the opening act of a play that many do not see the end too. But if you can ride that incredible wave, if you can stay balanced whilst the storms of normality are hurled at you and your relationship, then you have the chance of that love.

And it is the meaning of life.

I love you.

1 PANDER

God created mankind in his own image according to the Bible.

It wasn't his finest hour was it, let's be honest.

Not only did he do that but he also created a whole planet and put Adam onto it first. That's going to give anyone an inflated sense of importance right there, it is some magnificent present to receive.

"Here you go Adam, you are not getting socks for Xmas you are getting Earth"

Man's ego was thus created in one supernova flash of masculine ego fuelled lightning.

Adam duly arrived on his planet and immediately started to be all Godlike because, well, that is what God initially wanted. As each million years then passed by, through generation after generation of ancestors, through centuries of war, man continued to believe in his own self-importance.

As for the real God? What did he think? What did he do when he realised he had messed up?

Within seconds of creation, he came to the very sound conclusion that he had already overestimated man's capabilities and so he created Eve to sort them out.

Fast track 1 billon years and nothing much has changed at all.

Women are by far the more intelligent sex and in today's society, as man's self-proclaimed "power" declines, we are hopefully now seeing the last phase of an unequal dynamic between those sexes. In reality though, rather than women supposedly "catching up" with man, it is mankind who should be catching up with women, in the way they act, deal with issues and tackle the most important values in a relationship.

In this book, I am going to explain what goes on in mankind's often empty head, how they view things, how they go about their thought process and how they look at their wives and girlfriends. In doing so, I'm going to break man's secret oath, which is simply and intelligently described as *"what is said in the pub stays in the pub"*.

I like to think this makes me a super grass of the courageous and noble kind, not a snitch that will get banned from every pub in the country.

The biggest and most important thing though to do before we begin this journey of mankind enlightenment together is to get straight to the bleeding obvious.

Men and Women are different. We are different not only physically but emotionally too.

Of course, in things like rights, pay, equality etc. both sexes should absolutely be equal and indeed there is a strong argument for women to have a far greater slice than mankind. But emotionally and physically, men and women are not the same. That's a fact. Physically we accept that I think, equestrian is the only Olympic sport where men and women compete together, football teams are kept separate in the World Cup, Wimbledon has different competitions for the sexes it's a common thing.

It's just the way it is, physically men are born differently and that has been the reason mankind has been so "dominant" in the last million years because they have bullied their way into that position simply through the size of their bodies.

What we forget though is emotionally we are different too. Men will not react the same way to hundreds of everyday life issues and they won't think the same with regards relationships either. They communicate differently with their friends; they prioritise things differently and the sexes are like a square and a circle they both won't fit into the same hole society wishes it would.

There is no point in us pretending otherwise. Even down to the basic things we see things differently, simple tasks like keeping the house tidy. For example, a man would love to cook for his wife but by agreeing to this a lady is often opening up Pandora's juxtaposition box. Whilst she would be amazed at the dream of him making that "effort", equally, she will dread the thought of what state the kitchen will be in after he has finished.

Men have perfected the art of what is essentially known as *sweep and hide*. When he has finished using the food mixer, cutting the vegetables and grating the cheese he will look down at the floor and be genuinely surprised to see more laying down there than in the bowl on the kitchen table top.

Off he will go to get the hoover but when he tries to use the vacuum cleaner it is obviously already full and, frankly, he would have no idea how to empty or unblock it anyway. He reverts back to all he knows therefore, all he has ever been taught to do, all he is capable of which is just to throw it back into the cupboard, not with the wires neatly wrapped around the holding peg but with them in such a tangled mess that even the knotted-up Xmas lights would hold their head in utter shame.

With 5 minutes to go before his wife comes home, he is then faced with the ultimate dilemma. Does he tidy up properly not allowing him enough time to run upstairs and pour half a bottle of aftershave over every part of his body, or does he just kick all the mess on the floor under the fridge and congratulate himself on yet another mankind masterstroke.

Go look under your fridge now with a torch.

Told you so.

Women, so research has shown, go through 6 hormonal changes in their lives and men just mature a little bit, or not as the case may be. Emotions are different. Bodies are different. Hormones are different. Men don't experience child birth or the change of life. We have little comprehension on what that is like for a lady and how that could affect them.

I'm going to tell you the hard truth about mankind in this book. I'm not going to tell you what society wants you to hear. I'm going to explain why they act as they do, what they say and what they lie about in a language striped down to its very basics, which will cover all topics no matter how sensitive they are. This is warts and all and there is no hiding from it.

So, let's begin....

Once upon a time, all you wanted was the fairy-tale you had been promised by Walt Disney. The one where you fall for your hero, the man that you could only imagine ever having in unreachable dreams, a Romeo and Juliet romance which would last in your captivated heart for the rest of eternity.

You meet him for the first time.

He is handsome and confident, yet at the same time homely, calm, funny and as each minute passes more and more intriguing. You search for any sign of his thoughts, any interest in you, any indication that he may be already thinking emotionally what you are thinking.

As the minutes pass by you watch as he is silent occasionally for just a few seconds, starring into space, but it isn't an uncomfortable feeling, it is a mesmerising silence as his mind wanders to the place you want his thoughts to be in.

Which you really hope are about you.

You talk and talk and then you find yourselves almost alone. Except this isn't a movie where it is midnight and you are in a New York bar with the waiter looking frustrated at your happiness, it is the first date and the Gods are already deciding on your future. The setting is irrelevant, the butterflies gathering in your body simply do not care where you are in that beautiful moment.

At the end, you don't want to go. You hope he doesn't want to leave either. But you both walk out nonetheless because what is the right thing to do here? Say to him "*I am cancelling all my plans, I want to spend the rest of the week with you*"? How keen should you be? Do you play it cool or do you play it straight?

And then that moment comes. The goodbye. For a split second there is a pause. There is always a split-second pause on a first date as you leave each other.

The *"should we kiss?"* pause.

And, of course you shouldn't as, well, that wouldn't be right. But in that split second, the sensible spark that should stay within, is often hopelessly ignited and frankly you both can't help yourselves.

And if the Gods are with you, then that kiss will be the greatest of all time.

Of course, nothing is ever as Disney told us it would be, but God those opening moments and weeks of your relationship. Remember? The excitement of getting messages after you leave each other, the build-up to the next date, the first kiss, the romance, the intrigue, the desire on both sides to just please each other, the beautiful moments, the future plans you make when you know you really like each other. Mostly though it is having those goddamn beautiful butterflies in your stomach which reach your very soul again and again at the thought of being with each other forever.

That is magic right there, the most wonderful kind of emotional magic.

During those opening weeks and months, you learn about each other but equally both sides will still keep things close to their chests. Studies say we only reveal about 30% of our true selves at the most formative time of a relationship and that will usually be just the good stuff of course as we have a desire to impress.

To fall in love.

But when you go for a job, not only do you have to write out a CV and no doubt get interviewed several times, it is becoming more frequent that companies will adopt psychological profiling as well, including reviewing all your social media to see if you would culturally fit within their organisation. If you buy a house, you will do a survey and more often than not get guarantees that the place is as you thought it was. Local searches are done, tests are carried out on the health of the building and you walk around the local area again and again to see if you would be comfortable living there

Yet we make decisions at the start of a relationship based entirely on excitement and lust. We make decisions on individual people, not what their bodies represent. Men don't study women and women don't study men we assume we have that part covered because we are both humans, but we absolutely do not know about the differences between mankind/ women DNA because we are never taught it and we don't think to ever seek that knowledge.

The most powerful emotion you will ever have in your life is love. Love for your children you have immediately and you would step in front of a train to save them. Love for another human you have to build yourself, you have to maintain it and yet we are blinded and fooled by the thought that the palace of love will hold firm forever.

But buildings fall down, they develop cracks, require maintenance, require a change in decoration and so do relationships.

One life isn't always One love.

How well do you know mankind? You buy a car because it looks good, its practical, it has certain benefits and if it goes wrong, you get a mechanic. In a relationship you have to learn about the "car", the "engine" yourself because there is no one to subcontract that task out to.

As your child grows up they require different things at different ages which you adapt to and accept it willingly as you love them. Yet do you adapt in a relationship? Do you know how to adapt? Do you know enough about how mankind changes to even be able to? And, of course, vice-versa.

That is the real test of love.

Getting to the route of the problem right away, there are marriage counsellors but there aren't mankind counsellors. There isn't a Man Love Doctor to help you. You don't learn about mankind at school, though it would be an easy subject at that stage if you did because of the stereotype man has created for himself.

In basic language if you made an equation of how to understand a lady, something like this would represent the findings after years of Harvard University study:

$$W = a_0 + \sum_{n=1}^{\infty} \left(a_n \cos \frac{n\pi x}{L} + b_n \sin \frac{n\pi x}{L} \right)$$

Which essentially means it's impossible to break down how to understand a lady because they are too intelligent and are driven by successfully tackling multiple issues daily which will quite rightly affect their mood and their attitude to their partner.

For a man, the equation, after one minute of research would be

M = K

Where K = he makes all the decisions in his life on what his knob tells him to do.

Essentially the whole game between man and women has appeared for centuries to be based upon one word. However, whilst I agree that most of the illogical decisions a man makes in his life are driven by his penis, all is not as it seems with regards "sex" and why it is important.

It is so much deeper than that and more complex than just the feeling from 10 seconds of an orgasm. He gets more than 10 seconds of enjoyment from a lovely meal, by watching his kids, from winning a game of football, from laughing, from having a couple of pints but he isn't "ruled" by the pleasure they give him.

I'm going to explain in this book why that sexual 10 seconds is so important and if you can unlock that code, and the wider implications it has, it will then give you more of an understanding of the Meaning of Man. Mankind has these core inner values which define him and what he therefore needs to function emotionally.

P*roud*

A*ppreciated*

N*eeded*

D*esired*

E*nthusiastic*

R*espected*

Which spells "***PANDER***" and that is probably one of the most accurate acronyms ever created. Pandering to a man is what females have probably done since time began, not by choice but by tradition and it is only now you get the sense that relationship evolution is finally shifting. It will take another generation for elements of Pander to get to the right balance but nonetheless this is what has defined mankind. I don't say you should pander to the pander I simply point out this is inside him, what you do with that magical knowledge is entirely up to you. Some of these values, maybe all of them exist in women too, and you deserve the same back as you give your partner. This is key, this book is about man but you of course need a version of Pander too and without that then we are back to square one again in the totally outdated man v women balance that has existed in the last 1,000 years.

So, what I'm about to say is absolutely not a one-way street at all, if you give him "*PANDER*" then he should be giving back "*PANDER +++*" back and if he isn't, then tell him to shove his *PANDER* up his egotistical backside.

Men are insecure. The outward bravado is often a caricature of the real person underneath the utter nonsense that comes out of his mouth, especially when he is with his friends. So, he needs affirmation from his partner, he needs to feel that she is proud of him, when he is deserving of that, he needs to feel appreciated for what he does and wants to feel that he is enthusiastically needed in the relationship. He is well aware that women cope better being alone than he does.

Men need to feel respected. If they feel inadequate, privately or publicly then they can't function. Men thrive when they know their wives/partners admire and believe in them. They can't stand the thought of being humiliated which extends also to their chats with men. The respect from his lady is needed both publicly and privately and nothing is more important to him than that.

Men are afraid that if they aren't cutting it at home, then they have seriously diminished their use in the relationship. This is particularly true for example if they have lost their job. They also want to be desired by their partners, which is often a greater need than the act of sex itself.

When a man is rejected sexually or physically, he feels he is emotionally rejected too. To spark his emotional attachment quickly, you must ignite his sexual one. It's like a car which has run out of battery if you want to get it going again you will need to fire it up.

It is only through understanding the *PANDER* values and how that intertwines through man's daily life that you will then understand why your man does what he does and more so help you when things hit trouble. Now I'm generalising here but women will call their friends in times of a relationship crisis. A lot. They will read relationship articles written by women, never men, and the newspapers are full of them. All programs on TV about stuff like that are with women panelists, think *Loose Women*.

Women giving advice to women about men. In good faith sure, but that is the biggest mistake in the whole history of relationships over thousands of years. Because men are not the same and by some margin and it is my job now to convince you of that.

To make any sense of your relationship at any stage you have to delve into a man's brain and know what he thinks, before you act. Asking advice from your friends is pointless as they will, of course and understandably, see it from a lady's point of view only. But a man's mind only makes sense to a man and the real problem is it probably doesn't make any sense to him either.

The cliché that is always said is that *a way to a man's heart is through his stomach* but it simply isn't. It is through those *PANDER* values combined.

Proof?

Well, God forbid he cheats on you, it is not because someone else has offered to cook him a nice homemade pie with a side of spinach.

2 NONSENSE

Bollocks.

Now admittedly that's not the greatest opening to a chapter and one that you will not find in any Shakespearian play, but it is an important word nonetheless in your admirable and noble quest to understand mankind.

Every man has one skill, a talent that sets him apart from 4 billion other people on the planet e.g. ladies and it is something that they are all completely and utterly world class at.

Talking complete and utter pointless bollocks for hours and hours.

I'm going to reveal to you now for the first time ever, probably, what bollocks are discussed in the inner sanctum of mankind's world. My qualifications for this wisdom, aside from being a man, the hours of interviews I have done, the results of various personal surveys I have carried out and the review of endless reports prepared by others online, is that I had a "famous" man cave for a few years where both celebrities, famous snooker players and the masses congregated for hours on end.

And we all talked complete and utter pointless nonsense there for those hours on end.

"The Man Cave" is a phrase recognised throughout the world. There are 1.8 billion (yes billion) entries in google if you type those words in. Think about that for a moment. It has the word "cave" in it for a start which often gets overlooked but of course has a deeper meaning in that it refers to "cavemen" who were around over 25,000 years ago. I guess they were seen as the ultimate man's man, the tough hunter/gatherer who would bash anything on the head, not to eat but to impress the wife when he returned home with half a pterodactyl over his muscled shoulder.

Digressing for a just a moment, that does put 21st century man into humiliating shame though doesn't it. We moan about carrying two bags of shopping to the car, expecting huge amounts of praise as a result, whereas mankind's ancestors dragged a dinosaur 8 miles home and only stopped to eat one of its legs when he got a little bit peckish.

Thousands of years later, the place of gathering "exclusively" for men is still called a cave because it allows them to pretend they are still as "powerful" as they once were, until that is, it's time to leave that cave. Then they will once again enter the real world and accept where the true "power" sits and apologise profusely to their wives and girlfriends for being 10 minutes late and stinking of beer.

Neanderthal mankind is still out there though but a different species has evolved over the years, one which is more suited to the modern-day era. In my man cave, in they would all come like glorious peacocks, strutting to the beat of the bollocks that came out of their mouths every single second, hour, day, month and year I had that "arena".

Cave man meet Peacock. Evolution is a strange thing though. If a caveman had seen a peacock strutting away, out the wooden club would have come again and half an hour later the family would be eating it for supper.

A peacock's feathers are apparently among the most well-known examples of mating displays in the entire animal kingdom. They often carry out a form of courtship dance with an extravagant display, highlighting their magnificence as they walk around, trying to impress others, needing to stand out from the crowd. Which is exactly what men do generally in life and even more so in a masculine environment like a man cave. They try it with their appearance, their jokes, their banter, the way they compete against each other.

There is actually a term for it and it's called "Peacocking". I could spend the next ten minutes describing that to you in some sort of impressively deep psychological way but to speed things up, as I know you want to get to the sex bit of the book, simply think Mick Jagger.

On stage.

The Peacock Peacocking.

In that man cave many jokes were told. But there wasn't one serious occasion when anything misogynistic was said and we would not have tolerated it if it was.

It was a tongue in cheek environment and banter does still happen. Mankind is still learning to evolve in that way as we have a familiarity with jokes about women, but as I'm sure ladies do about men. In fairness, we did all accept what complete idiots we were in the man cave and over a 3-year period, hundreds and hundreds of men gathered there. It was quite a big place next to the main house with a bar, snooker table, darts all the things you could imagine we would need to be "men". But as I listened to everyone, at an early stage I knew I would write a book on mankind because whilst I am not denying I got involved in some of the nonsense, so did barristers, doctors, teachers, warehousemen, plumbers, publishers, salesman, accountants and from every walk of life you could imagine aged between 20 to 70.

There is no comparable place as such like a man cave for ladies to "gather". Why? Well, they don't need a man cave they are rational and civilized humans. They don't strut around like peacocks because they don't need a caricature of themselves, they are comfortable with who they already are.

Women 1 Peacocks 0.

A pub in the old days, could certainly be described as a "man cave" and in certain areas of the UK, like in Newcastle, they still exist in the sort of way they always were. It is traditional still for the Geordie men on a Sunday to be dropped off by their wives/girlfriends for the afternoon of men only chat, nonsense and gambling at the local boozer. But the interesting thing here is, from discussions I have had with their partners, is that the ladies are very happy to drop them off because they get some peace and quiet for once. There is no feeling that this is the return of male chauvinistic 18th century abuse, merely an understanding that some traditions of man/women behaviour are still ok and I guess that's a good thing.

Most of men's verbal bollocks cover 3 areas. Women, sport and competition. In doing so they will use often use exaggeration as the peacock's jockey for acceptance. To highlight my point, let's take a basic and fairly obvious question which will be asked by both man and woman at some point in a relationship I'm sure.

How many people have you slept with?

If a man answers that same question to his friends, he will lie but to you he will also lie. And he will often lie to himself. There can't be many subjects that everyone will lie about but this is defiantly one of them.

If and when that question arises, whatever he says to his friends you can generally take off anywhere between a third and a half to get to the right answer. When a man answers that question to you, generally add another 100%

So

1) (To men) "*yep I must have had 30 by now mate and they all loved it*", is actually translated as "*yep I have actually had sex with 14 ladies and with most I was probably useless*"

2) (To you) "*Baby I probably have only had 12 partners*" is translated as he has had at least 24.

They may occasionally take time off from talking nonsense (a bollocks sabbatical) but put them in front of their old school friends with two pints of lager inside them, with no women around, and out those verbal bollocks come again to say hello.

He will swear a lot with when he is with his friends. It becomes the default language no matter how clever he is. He could have taught physics at Cambridge University during the day, comparing Einstein's Theory of Relativity with Newtons Law of Motion, but when he arrives into the pub that night with the rest of mankind he will simply say

"******* hell, what a ****" on repeat before he goes home.

A man's bollocks are usually full of juvenile retorts and anecdotes that he will continually repeat throughout his whole life. For example, one of the more common phrases the dominant male of the peacock pack will utter, is "*I would*" as a lady walks past and quite often that ever so funny outburst will get "*I already have*" as a reply from one of his friends, making everyone around chuckle in masculine merriment at the joke they have heard a million times.

They have missed the point though. She never would with them, ever.

Men rarely talk about their current girlfriends/wives in any depth with anyone and I guess the most important thing to note on this is that for 94% of the time (according to my private survey) they will never talk about their sex life with them either. And that bizarrely is respect, a strange type of respect I give you that but it is none the less. I would have said that % would have been 99% because I have never known any situation when someone has told me about anything they do with their "serious" partner and for 3 years in that man cave not once did I hear of any description about anything on that subject.

That is mainly out of "respect" but also a fear of anyone "fancying" their partners too much if they described how amazing they were in bed or what they did or what they dressed like. I have never seen one "naughty" picture or "video" of anyone's wives that I knew and 88% of people in my survey confirmed that too.

On an emotional level, a man won't discuss his feelings or his love. If the question comes to a man, *"how's Jane?"* the sort of reply would be bland *"great thanks"*, it will never be *"my god she is so amazing mate, I am so in love it hurts like hell"*. You will get "pride" in say a discussion to do with work or a hobby or an achievement but you won't get pride in the sense of *"went out for dinner last night and she wore this black dress and Jesus she looked so beautiful"* he would rather put that picture on social media than describe it to others.

Men, on the whole, regarding ladies are visual and high level. According to the studies, women over think about relationships, men under think.

However, on the sporting level, this is where it would simply astonish you how detailed men are. When a lady asks him a simple question at home about anything he can often be evasive and generalise but when it comes to Man Utd v Liverpool in May 1984 he can real off the tactics, the goals, the man of the match and what pie he ate at half time as the banter goes back and forth in a discussion they have probably had before but need to relive again for no other reason than it continues the bollocks.

Within mankind's nonsense chats with other men, there is a deep-rooted pride in anything they have achieved in their lives. He is quite happy to repeat the story of those achievements again and again and anything he wins at against his mates, be it a game of golf, snooker, darts or monopoly, he thrives at relieving it.

Most men I interviewed reported back though that their partners approached these "achievements" in a dismissive way, as inconsequential, which they no doubt are in the grand scheme of life, but actually they aren't. Remember the *PANDER* values at all times.

An example.

Your man plays golf. Do you know what his best score was? I bet you he is damn proud of that score. When he gets in from golf, you might say *"did you have fun?"* and possibly *"did you win"* as an afterthought. But say you asked him what his score was and was there a hole he felt he could do better at? That is *PANDER* and he will definitely notice it.

The biggest bit of bollocks I have ever heard though arrived into my ears when I wrote Lizzie Cundy's book with her. She is probably the most well-connected lady in the UK with Tom Cruise, Al Pacino, Leonardo DI Caprio and other people of that magnitude in her very impressive address book.

This also included Mickey Rourke the Oscar nominated Hollywood Hellraiser. He told her that in one single night he had slept with 14 women. Now bear in mind that most men would struggle to last 14 minutes with one girl let alone all night with 14 women, many many women she told that story to believed it.

Every man on earth however knows that simply could not have happened or not in the way it is implied. Arise Sir Mickey, King of bollocks.

Mankind will often either downright lie about achievements or take an element of truth and exaggerate it. What may have been true is that he had a few girls back to his room that night. Let's give him the benefit of the doubt and say half his quota, 7. And he may well have had a good time with them all but he certainly did not cum more than say 4 times in an 8 hour stretch.

And every one of those men on earth would have been impressed at the story as I have just described it if it had been 7 ladies. He would have received God like status and be forever adored as a sexual icon for all of eternity. But being a typical man, that wasn't enough so he upped the bollocks and proclaimed that he had 14 women in one night.

And the story also shows up numerous flaws behind the bollocks, which there often is when analysed in the cold light of day. How would he have decided the order? Would he make number 14 to be the best or the worse? When you have dinner, you may leave the best part of the food until the end, so was 14 the best mouthful he wanted to have or just a number to boost, well, the numbers. Did he say to Miss 14 *"hurry up love my honey syrup waffles are about to arrive"* as the sunrise came up or did he stare into 14's eyes and say *"you are one I have been longing for all my life baby"*.

Or was say number 3 the best as he would have warmed up by then? Did the ladies know their number order? Or was 14 actually 14 in one go on a steel reinforced bed?

If someone went twice would that count as "1 go" or 2 in the 14. If there were twins was that 1 or 2 in the counter? How did he know it was 14 anyway, did he mark them off like he was playing bingo as the ladies left? How did he know their names? Was it like the Queen when the Palace butler whispers in her ear as the dignitaries file by? In Mikey's case was it a man appearing from under the bed saying *"That's Sharon Mikey"* as the next blonde walked into le boudoir?

And what about the linen? Were the sheets changed after each one? Were the hotel maids on standby outside? And when each left, did he have someone take a survey outside so he could improve on the performance he would give with the later numbers.

It could have been a multiple-choice type survey with a lady using a clipboard

"Tell me "Mikey 4" ….

How would you rate the conversation after sex this evening?

A) He was very loving and attentive

B) Not bad but seemed to be looking over my shoulder at the door a lot

C) Terrible with him but good with the maids as they changed the satin sheets after

D) What conversation, he jumped straight out of bed to watch Match of the Day

How would you describe the foreplay?

A) Attentive to my needs and made sure I had an equal share of the enjoyment

B) If foreplay is defined "as I did it all", then yes it was excellent

C) There was none whatsoever, he said sorry for the short delay but it had been a long night and as soon as he could get his knob to rise again could I jump on board and get it over with quickly as he had a target to reach.

But quite simply all these thoughts just leave one obvious conclusion to reach.

He was talking absolute mankind bollocks.

3 RESPONSIBILITY

Laughter

… would be the undoubted response from 99.99% of all wives or partners if their "man" said he were going to take their child on holiday by himself.

And I can understand why that would be such a comedy moment.

Imagine your partner having to arrange the beach bag on holiday. Whereas you would (the night before) have carefully packed the sun cream, the bee sting lotion, the antihistamines, headache pills, sunglasses, sunglass wipes, book, spare book, after sun, beach towels, sun hats, bottles of water, pool games, fruit and phone battery recharger, he will just wake up late and frankly not pack any of the above as he didn't actually realise you needed a beach bag, that it would just magically appear by his sun lounger just like when "things" get done round the house by the magic fairy too.

Man is a great believe in that magic fairy.

And when at 4pm on day one of the father/child holiday he suddenly realises that the shade of pink on his son cheeks isn't a spilt cherry ice crush drink it is in fact sunburn as he forgot to put sun cream on the 7 year old, the only thought in his mind is not to get the after sun on, it is to quickly bribe his child £20 to take the wrap when you video call him that night.

"Sorry Mummy, Daddy was so great today it's just I wiped the cream off after he had put it on because it itched" little Jonny will say in dimmed lights so you can't see the blisters starting to form on his face.

Men are just not as organised or as practical as women. They are so often just one-dimensional thinkers. Multi-tasking in their minds consists of holding a beer in one hand and talking total rubbish all at the same time.

To highlight this, 69% of all women apparently still do the weekly food shopping. I would like to think this isn't an indication of mankind hanging onto centuries of misogynistic undeserved "power" but more a reflection instead of the fact that men will get it totally wrong if they volunteered to do it.

Let's face it, the only chance he would have if he did head to the supermarket would be if a list, written by you, accompanied him. And that's my point, you cannot trust him to think logically. You need to spell it out. As a by-product, the way to tell if a man is married or not isn't to see if he has a wedding ring on, it is to notice if he has a list in his hand as he pushes the trolley around the cold food section of the local Sainsbury's.

Which of course is a total disaster waiting to happen with or without that list.

You send him off to Tesco's. When he eventually gets back it will have taken him twice the amount of time it would have taken you. And that is at best. He will have ambled down the aisles, getting confused over which potatoes are best, getting distracted by the pork pies, and then on aisle 34 a mirage of wonder will have appeared before him which is of course the booze section. When he should still be in aisle 4, the home of healthy yoghurt, he will spend at least the next 20 minutes staring at the lager cans wondering how many he can get actually get away with buying, despite the fact it only says 4 cans (double underlined) on the instructions you have written to him.

Your list will also undoubtedly say "toilet roll" but the lack of any further helpful information will totally confuse him. Mankind has never considered how "soft" they need to be in his life and certainty not if they should be "luxury soft". He won't understand what "double quilted" is, let alone even ponder the need for fresh, sensitive, flushable, moist toilet wipes. And in that desperate moment when he stares at shelf upon shelf of rolls he knows there is no one who can help, he cannot call his mates because of the ridicule that will last for all eternity if he does and he is totally determined to not call you because it that will show just how pathetic a man actually is.

Once again.

All that however is a warm up to the main event which is mankind's stroll down aisle 31, otherwise known as the walk of shame. Or to put it another way, the washing powder aisle. Fabric conditioner? Is that really essential?

The list just says washing powder but does that mean powder or detergent? Does it mean capsules? Does it mean extra stain removal all in one capsules? What is the difference? Why is there a difference? Is a bit of dirt an actual stain?

But when he does eventually return to the house, he will believe he has all the things on the list you have given him, so much so that he proudly displays that herculean good deed all over the kitchen table for your inspection and approval.

There is a pause though.

An uncomfortable one.

You look at him, he looks at you. Eyes on eyes. Then those fateful words arrive from your scornful lips

"You didn't get the eggs"

Eggs?? Flustered ever so slightly panicking, heart racing, your man looks down at the list and they are not there, no mention of them at all. Because to you, *naturellement*, it's just common sense that a list is a guideline, but to a man he can't think multi-dimensionally and especially in a supermarket. It's the list he was working too. How was he to know you sent him to Tesco for bread, milk, sugar, beans and wine but what you actually expected was for him to return home with £300 of shopping which would last at least 2 months.

To make matters worse sometimes, as you know he will ask for a list, the more vicious ladies amongst you (so basically 99.999%) will put something on there which will totally embarrass him because this is one opportunity to get back at mankind for thousands of years of his self-proclaimed over importance.

"Baby can you go to the shops for me" you purr like Cleopatra herself, lulling your man into a false sense of security

"Yes honey, of course" man replies because that will mean he will be in your good books with the slight possibility therefore that sex will be offered that evening as the well-deserved "reward"

But then this comes from the lips of the she devil herself

"Eggs, milk, bread and lube please darling"

And with a gulp, an oh bollocks gulp, off he will go.

He has to get it now as it's on the list and that is like a legal contract between man and women. He has a strategy though, the same one he used to adopt when he went into the supermarket to buy condoms when he was 18. He will walk past the health products section the lube is in slowly, coolly, calmly, whistling, To the other people in the shop it sounds like a flock of birds has arrived as other men are in the same aisle, walking slowly, coolly, calmly, whistling, it's a set drill central to their DNA. Then when the coast is clear e.g. no shop assistants or other ladies in sight he will double back and not looking at all at the products but staring ahead, his hand will suddenly reach out and grab whatever lube he can in double quick time before quickly placing it under something else in the trolley.

He has never been so stressed in his life but he makes it home, and he has the lube but with the overriding thought that it could have been a lot worse.

You could have asked for Tampax as well.

Now that is a subject, to our utter shame, no man wants to hear.

But they should do.

Periods, the monthly menstrual cycle. Mankind's view on this subject is to close ranks and sympathise with each other when the words my wife/partner is "on" comes out of their mouths. That high chaparral of compassion is not for the lady though, and what she may be going through, the only thing that has just entered mankind's head is that "period" means their partner is likely to be moody, temperamental and short tempered as a consequence.

I'm writing this definition now for the men who are reading the book. A period happens because of changes in hormones flowing through the body. They are chemical messengers and the ovaries release hormones, estrogen and progesterone to showcase it. These cause the lining of the uterus to build up, ready for a fertilized egg to attach and start developing. If there is no fertilized egg, the lining breaks down and bleeds.

Then the same process happens all over again the next month and continues for decades.

Not once have I ever heard men discuss what I have just put into words and in my survey 88% of men could not describe what exactly a period was either. Not only that, 93% said they had never actually discussed it with their partner, what they go through and how to help them. And yet that "event" happens every month, every year for c35 years and we never discuss it. The only thing that enters our head is to feel sorry for ourselves that we are at the brunt of the short temperedness and even more selfishly, that our sex life may be on hold for a week because of it.

It is completely shameful, that such a change of hormones in our partners is only seen as an inconvenience to our lives not how it affects them at all.

Not only do ladies have to cope with that, they also have pregnancy to deal with, should that occur of course. And in some ways, the same mindset in mankind on periods I'm afraid extends also to child birth and labour. Let's face up to it, men cannot give birth physically but they could also probably not go through it mentally either. They simply cannot comprehend what a lady has to endure with childbirth and that it takes extraordinary mental toughness to live through that and the after effects on emotions, hormones and their way of life.

Mankind's involvement in those 9 months effectively starts and ends with sex.

That's it.

Men on the whole do not understand anything in detail about childbirth. If you asked him to describe the process of pregnancy from start to finish, the hormonal changes, what happens when the baby turns inside a lady's stomach, the risk of high blood pressure during pregnancy on life itself, the water breaking, the feeling of contractions, how long contractions last for, what it feels like to "push the baby out", what emotions a woman goes through immediately after birth and the possibility of post-natal depression for months after, he would score zero.

And that would be on a good day.

And I would have been amongst those scoring zero. It was only because of this book I started to listen to stories about pregnancy and childbirth. Over the years, I thought I was quite understanding generally about it all, as I have two children, about the process and the after birth process. As much as I could I mucked in with baby duties during the night with both my children and I guess thought that was my job done.

But I had never in my whole life asked detailed questions about childbirth and pregnancy and, of course, after a while as the kids grow up the chances of that discussion happening fall away. This is even more astonishing for me as when my daughter was born, my wife at the time became seriously ill with high blood pressure which escalated into a severe life or death situation. An emergency caesarean was carried out at 39 weeks which led to her being rushed into intensive care for a week.

I remember going up in the lift to the ICU unit just after birth as they tried to get needles into her veins, asking the doctors if she would live or die and they just couldn't tell me.

She did survive, but to my shame when my second child was born, I still didn't research pregnancy, the risks and everything described above. I have thought long and hard about that in countless periods of recent self-reflection and there are only two sensible answers to it;

- Pregnancy and childbirth produce no *PANDER* values in mankind. We quite rightly aren't *desired* at all from start to finish, we won't be *appreciated*, it is going to be damn tricky for a lady to be *enthusiastic* about us when she is going through labour and whilst we may be *needed*, it will be in a low-level practical kind of way like shopping which we are all useless at anyway.

- Mankind know that women at the end of the day cope so well, they seem always in control, they get on with things without question and therefore it makes man blind to the whole process. I guess there is a sense, certainly with me, that I took that stuff for granted. Because women handle things so well, we don't treat the understanding of it as a priority and yet the "trauma" of birth and the 9 months of pregnancy beforehand will of course affect a woman mentally forever. Even the simplest of things like having a drink of wine to relax can't be done for 9 months. Mankind couldn't even cope with that let alone the rest of it.

To make matters worse during pregnancy, not only do men not understand it or talk about it they will occasionally give a roll of the eyes in a "I'm hard done by way" look to their friends

But men do love their children. They adore their children. In the thousands of conversations, I have had with them over the years the only time they are not talking nonsense is when they discuss their kids. They are proud of them, they are excited to see them and whilst a mother of course has developed her attachment through carrying the child inside her for 9 months, it doesn't mean the love a man has for his children is any less than hers.

That love for a child is equal amongst parents but there is a simple fact of God/evolution which is that only women can give birth, only they can carry that unborn baby in their body for 9 months. There is a reason for it. Think about it.

It is because men could not cope. We struggle to cope practically on any level where our children are concerned. If we babysit, as long as we know the child is in the same house as us that counts as job done. God forbid there is any small emergency we are in big trouble, but yet we will still never call another man for help or advice, there is pride at stake.

"Mate, I'm here with Billy and his nappy is overflowing, he is crying non-stop and has a tiny rash on his bum what do I do?" is never coming out of any man's mouth.

In cases like these there are two mankind default positions. Google the problem and then when that fails, it is to just reach for the Calpol bottle and quickly pour the legal maximum amount into our child's mouth before going back downstairs to watch the football.

Along the same lines, if 99.99% of women would laugh out loud if their partner suggested taking their child on holiday with him, 100% would laugh if he suggested that he wrapped the presents for his children at Xmas instead of you. Men and wrapping paper are not a match made in any heaven. Whereas you will no doubt carefully fold the edges, cut the lines with a ruler, make sure the sellotape is exactly the correct length after having spent at least half an hour in the shop ensuring the paper is the right colour and design in the first place, he will just shove the present on a table, fold any bit of wrapping paper he found in the cupboard over it, hurl reams of sellotape around the middle and with an encore worthy of his own stupidity, make no attempt whatsoever to cover around the bits he missed in the naive hope you wouldn't notice it.

This Xmas responsibility of leaving man to his own devices also extends to the present he has got you. Frankly the only thing you care about when you open his gift on Christmas Day is where the receipt is as apparently one in three ladies will return the gifts their partner buys them.

Thankfully, though, you are not totally innocent here ladies in your choice of presents for man. An online survey in the USA set out the top 5 things ladies like to buy their partners and it highlights the flaws in your buying pattern too.

You have to remember men are simple and easily pleased you don't need to overcomplicate what you buy for him. The top 5 were

1) Wine paraphernalia

This would include things like a wine book, or a fancy corkscrew all wrapped up in magnificent wrapping paper and bows no doubt for mankind's artistic and visual delight.

Right subject, wrong present. The clue was there all along, hiding in plain sight: men like wine and beer so just get him some and watch him happily guzzle it whilst he watches Match of the Day in a Saturday night mankind daze of plutonic happiness.

2) Driving gloves

I can understand why to you they reflect a vision of an Aston Martin convertible, winding through mountain roads with timeless glamour and style. But your man isn't Daniel Craig, he drives a Ford through B-roads and no amount of leather around his hands will ever change that.

3) A Wallet

As creatures of habit, men will like their current wallet. The leather has grown reassuringly soft and there's a slot for everything needed. The new one will inevitably be too big or small, with annoying pockets and creaky leather. In any case a new wallet it a total waste of money as within a week he will be out with his friends and it would therefore have been on the table in a shallow pool of lager for 2 hours.

4) A Posh new shaving kit

You know the ones, they have a shiny little stand, a goat's hair shaving brush, a platinum-bladed razor together with a new apothecary jar of holistic shaving foam. The thing is, men have been shaving every day for years and have a set routine for how they do it. if it's too complicated you are more likely to get a man to not shave at all which is fine if you want one of the guitar players from ZZ top to snog you but not if you object to a rash every time a beard is rubbed against your soft and ageless cheeks.

5) An experience

Generally, this would be a cool thing to get for a man but rather than a trip around a racing track in a sports car, more often than not he will receive from you a falconry or archery experience in the New Forest. Think basic not new age.

As further evidence of my very sound conclusion about men and responsibility, there is a TV show called "Don't tell the bride" where the wedding is organised by the man and he has a fixed budget to spend presumably given by the TV company in return for the bride and grooms involvement. A good idea at first sight I'm sure, as weddings can be very expensive but utter madness if you wanted to get the day of your dreams.

That program sums up this chapter in one hour of TV mankind "magic". The show is not only comedy gold it validates my theories on mankind totally as the viewers watch in open mouthed utter astonishment as soon as the groom starts to plan the big day.

And these are proper weddings. They actually are going to get married.

Particular highlights included the groom blowing half the overall budget on the stag night leaving virtually nothing for the wedding dress. Both he and the best man actually thought that the wedding dress wasn't even in the top 5 things of importance they needed to spend the money on.

That episode was nothing though compared to the one where the guy decided an alien theme was very appropriate for the most important day in his fiancé's life. There she was expecting to walk down the aisle looking like Princes Diana and instead she arrived as a green monster from the planet ZOG.

Which brings up the wider issue of clothes from the whole debacle that TV show opened up the door to. If you went shopping for your man it's a safe bet getting him some jeans and shirt would be OK. But if a man buys say a dress or shoes for you without any hint or clue in advance, there is no hope at all he will get it right. And when I say no hope, I mean with cast iron absolute and eternal certainty zero chance.

The engagement ring is a symbol of everlasting love and the most important thing a man could ever buy a lady.

And mankind knows it.

The results of a large survey in America stunningly declared that one in ten women would turn down the proposal of marriage if they didn't like the ring and one in three would actually return the ring and exchange it after the proposal.

Consider this. The day of the proposal arrives, he has arranged the most perfect setting, he has the roses, the champagne everything ready hidden around the corner for when you will both celebrate the happiest moment of your lives.

"*Baby will you marry me*" your knight in shining armour says, on one knee, holding your hand and staring at you with eternal love in his puppy dog eyes.

He hands you the ring box, lovingly touching your face as he does so

However according to that survey:

- 10 percent of you would now say to him "*Are you having a fucking laugh, is that what you really think of me ?!*" and storm off with a flat refusal to ever marry him.

- 30 percent of you would now say to him *"Err…Ok thanks…yes I suppose I will marry you but have you got the receipt still for that thing you assumed was a ring"*

Apparently though 52% of ladies would not say anything but deep down wished they had chosen it themselves. He can't even buy you the right skirt, how is he going to buy you the right ring? 40% of ladies have said that the ring to them symbolizes how much their man loves them and they judge him on that. So, he may be attentive, thoughtful, caring, kind, generous and romantic for years before the proposal but 4 ladies out of 10 thinks if he gets the wrong ring then he doesn't love you at all.

Beyoncé, in the song "All the single ladies" wrote a few words that has become a statement of intent for all womenkind

"if you liked it then you should have put a ring on it"

Which is absolutely true.

But in reality, he would have got the wrong ring to put on it anyway.

Our lack of ability to cope with child responsibility also raises doubts about our reliability when it comes to pets or any living thing that requires any form of attention.

I am going to tell you a story about me. I have an IQ of 143 which is Mensa level but I only say that to highlight that I am as idiotic as the rest of mankind in many many situations. Basic intelligence leaves us very quickly as you are about to find out.

A few years ago, I had been entrusted with looking after the fish and the birds one night as my second wife and my son had gone away for the weekend. How hard could that be? 3 small fish swimming around a tank and 2 birds in a cage. I didn't have to walk them, feed them, talk to them or even check if they were ok, this was the kind of responsibility that every man can only dream of.

I had been on my own all of 2 hours when I made the fatal mistake, which all men do, of wanting to impress his wife. This meant going further than the basic instruction given to me by her, 1 hour 59 minutes previously as she walked out the door, which was

"If there is a power cut then check if the pets are ok but apart from that don't even fucking look at them."

Ignoring that piece of helpful advice, I decided I would clean the bird cage and the fish tank which I had never done before. I had mastered the skill of always being busy when those moments arrived, but nonetheless I walked confidently into my son's room and there the two tiny budgerigars were, chirping away sitting on their porch as happy as they could be. I opened the little door to the cage, scooped up some of the mess at the bottom and as I turned to put it into the bin, those little sweet chirping fuckers sped past my hand like Concorde in a rush to get to New York City.

"Oh, fuck they actually do fly!" I screamed to no one but poor me as I hurled myself towards the bedroom door to keep them "trapped" into one space. They looked down from the top of the curtains, chirping away again without a care in the world.

It is here that the practical side of a lady would normally kick in. Instead, the illogical, idiotic tactics mankind adopts arrived into town once more.

I decided I would give the curtain a shake and by doing so the birds would decide freedom was actually overrated, and fly back to the safety of their cage. I convinced myself that for this to work, I must have the element of surprise, so I casually walked past whistling away, then I twisted like they did last summer, got carried away and instead of a gentle pull to dislodge them I yanked the curtains so hard that the whole thing came down, including the pole.

And then, as I lay there, the birds took the ultimate piss by pissing on me in their flight back to the cage where they just sat on top of it, chirping away again in their selfish lucky victory. I put my middle finger up to them as a sign of masculine superiority and carefully shut the door behind me deciding that task of "bird into cage" would be left to another time, a bit like the way mankind views washing up.

I made my way to the fish tank downstairs and googled how you clean it which apparently involved putting a suction hose into the tank, pump out a third of the water and then put in a new lot mixed with some chemicals.

Into the draw below the tank I went, found the long tube and started the suction process which meant pressing on a ball at the end of the pipe and the water would then start to travel along it into a bucket which I had set up.

My phone suddenly rang, it was my wife and I briefly walked away to get a better signal. 30 seconds later I returned to the room

"Of course, nothing is wrong here darling, Armageddon hasn't arrived, stop worrying"

I said to her as I confronted the Armageddon which had arrived in front of me. The four horses of the apocalypse were in my front room, watching as the water which had been flowing like the Nile on a summers evening only a minute before had now stopped. There was a blockage in the tube and that blockage happened to be my son's favourite fish, Pirate, a black and white goldfish he had spent an hour choosing just the week before.

Yep, nothing wrong here darling.

I ran around looking for some scissors to cut the tube and remembered there was a pair in my son's craft box in his room. I sped upstairs and grabbed them but as I desperately cut into the plastic tube, a few seconds later past my head flew those chirping birds once again. And for the ultimate crowd-pleasing effect, they did a u turn and flew past me for a second time as if they were the Red Arrows at the Farnborough summer air show.

I had of course left the door open to my son's room in my "pirate" panic. Not only that but as I cut through the tube, water had then started to flood out onto the floor.

I surveyed the scene. Definitely nothing wrong. Water chemical damage had now stained the carpet. A dead fish called pirate wasn't going to sing *"pieces of eight pieces of eight"* anytime soon, curtains and pole were in a heap upstairs and two free roaming birds were in front of me chirping away at my utter misfortune.

"If there was a power cut then check if they are ok apart from that don't even fucking look at them" she had said to me.

It's at this point mankind reverts to another default position, which is of course thinking about who else he can blame. When that doesn't work, he will then sulk and wonder why this could possibly have happened to him before heading to his local pub.

The ending to my pet story? Well, I eventually got the birds back into the cage but gave up on everything else. When my wife returned home early the next day, she opened the front door, took one look at me and immediately said before even looking around the house

"Ok, what the hell have you been up to?"

And I then did what any man would have done in that situation

"Fancy a trip to Selfridges baby, we can talk about it there?" I replied

There is one final reflection I want to make on all this. As women go through such tremendous pain during birth, it has set the tone for how they translate something which they assume is a man talking utter nonsense again but when he is, in fact, often not doing so at all.

It relates to the two most misunderstood words a man can ever say in a relationship. Since time began and over millions of years, these words have been treated with disinterest, suspicion and downright total and utter contempt by every single lady that has ever existed on planet earth.

And what could these two seemingly innocent letters uttered by mankind be?

"I'm ill"

And if those two words are doubled up into a foursome of utter stupidity with *"man flu"* added as well, then watch out mate because your women is going to chew you up and spit you out in a volcanic explosion of pure disdain.

I predict a riot.

And frankly, with what they have to deal with during pregnancy, who could ever blame them.

4 COMMUNICATON

13rd December 1992 changed relationships forever.

To save you the task of googling what this mysterious introduction means, that was the date of the first ever text message. Fast forward 20 years and the ability to now communicate across multiple different platforms, mainly through your phone, has without any doubt contributed towards the break down in marriages.

It makes cheating easier and communication more confusing.

Messages sent between partners can easily get misinterpreted and because they can be saved, it gives both parties the opportunity after an argument to read them again and again bringing a tit for tat frenzy of typing insults as a result.

Divorce rates in the 1960s were 2%, they are now 9%. Case closed.

We don't talk anymore we type or we swipe. We don't laugh with each other anymore we send emojis. We don't think about what we say anymore, autocorrect does that for us and we all hide behind WhatsApp, Instagram and Messenger in our everyday lives because it allows us to not face up to reality.

When you first meet someone, you send message after message, 20, 30+ a day but after a while you hit that horrible thing called normality and that's when that number turns into 3 (which is the average in a relationship apparently). At the same time, messages in the early days like *"can't wait to see you, I've got butterflies just thinking about it"* six months later turns into "*I will be home at 6, what's for dinner?*".

Mankind rarely show messages you have sent your partner to their friends. In fact, I can't recall any occasion where someone has forward to me a message or shown me anything face to face. On the whole men do not message a lot between themselves, banter is usually verbal it isn't WhatsApp to WhatsApp unless its' half time in a game of football they are watching.

Therefore, it is one of the first early signs of cheating if the amount of time your man is messaging on his phone noticeably increases.

Men notice that too. If someone in a "man crowd" starts to message a lot, everyone knows that is unlikely to be his wife/partner and he wouldn't be messaging other men either as he has the banter he needs in front of him at that very moment. A man doesn't like messaging his long-term partner when he is with his mates. They will ridicule him. But hypocritically, he does like a quick text when you are out with yours and many a row has been had because he doesn't get one, or indeed it isn't "nice enough".

An interesting part of the phone communication craze is the simple art of the message itself which carries all sorts of *battle of the sex's issues* and phycological insecurities.

A surprising result of my private survey was the issue of the number of "x" you put at the end of a message to your man. I have no idea if it is of any concern to ladies but it certainly seems to be to mankind, as is the time it takes for you to reply to a message and who messages first apparently.

It was said to me quite often that the "man view" is that he will often put one kiss less than the lady and he doesn't really want to go above 2. That survey I carried out privately, showed that 54% followed this general rule and 68% consciously thought when they sent a message how many "x" the reply "deserved".

So, as an example, if you sent a message to your man "*how are you baby xx*" he would reply "*great thanks x*". but if you sent "*how are you baby xxxx*" he would reply "*great thanks xx*" and not add the third "x" as the maximum is 2. Utterly astonishing I'm even writing this but that is society today. Blame Apple not me.

There also seems to be an issue with the time it takes for a man's partner to reply to a message he has sent.

Studies show 95% of messages will be read within 3 minutes of them being delivered, with the average response time being a mere 90 seconds. In America, 76% of men do not like it if their partner takes more than 20 minutes to reply to a message, when they know there is no reason not too e.g., you are not in any work meeting. As if a relationship wasn't complicated enough, now the timing of a reply to a simple message can cause a massive argument because to men, it shows a lack of respect, which is one of their core *PANDER* values.

It's all just a game of message tennis. The world is now message love at first read, not love at first sight. Not only do you have to be compatible physically and emotionally with your partner, you need to be compatible electronically as well.

Digital foreplay.

The stats are simply jaw dropping. Americans send 26 billion text messages a day. WhatsApp report that across the world, 65 billion messages are sent every 24 hours. 41% of what ladies use a mobile phone for is messaging (22% men) and women send 10 times more messages than calls (men 4 times).

Messaging can cause arguments, which even extends now to a row about not getting a message at all. Imagine that in the real world, arguing at home because you didn't talk to each other for an hour, or didn't give your partner enough kisses on the cheek as you left home that day, the world has gone crazy.

So, after setting the scene, let's get to the point of all this which is the way you digitally message your man is so vitally important. There are three types of texts, factual, emotional and sexual. (I will refer to them as texts even though of course it could be WhatsApp, Messenger etc),

Start with those *PANDER* values again which especially apply to emotional texts and when ever you want to say something of meaning I honestly recommend you refer back to those and shape the message around it. That's the absolute golden rule of digital mankind communication and if you are tempted at this point to shoot the messenger, I humbly once again ask (or plead, beg whatever you want, I have no shame) that you blame Apple for this digital debacle and not mankind's holy messenger (which is me).

Essentially this means avoiding the generic texts, the ones that are almost sent as a *"damn I need to text him let's just copy and paste one I did before"* kind, like

1) *"Miss you"*
2) *"I love you."*
3) Or even just *"Xxx"*

Instead, think about his core values and perhaps send ones like

1) *"Can't stop thinking about you today, just wanted you to know that."*
   "Thank you for always being there for me, I really don't know what I would do without you."
2) *"I hope you know how wonderful and great you are"*
3) *"Our relationship is so perfect, you are my King."*
4) *"I just want to be curled up in your arms right now and feel protected."*
5) *"I really really fucking miss you today"*.
6) *"You looked so handsome when I saw you this morning"*
7) *"All my friends are jealous of our relationship; they want a man like you"*
8) *"I'm so proud of you for getting that promotion."*

All these trigger *PANDER* and show you have actually thought about it. Again, I completely accept this is not a one way street and he better start showing you some of this back.

Turning to the grubby stuff e.g., sex texting, this will open up a can of worms but nonetheless I won't shy away from what mankind want and not what society believes it would want in a message. To highlight this, I found some examples online of what a lady columnist recommended you should send to your man and in return I have commented on what mankind would have really liked instead.

Of course, if you aren't comfortable with any sort of sexual message then absolutely you should not do it. It isn't a relationship or marriage deal breaker and nor should it ever be. I simply write the following to show the difference in thinking between the sexes once again and if you are going to do it, then do it to get the reaction you really want.

A lady columnist recommended you send to your man:

1) *"I love sitting on your ……"*

Open ended sentences in messages will not get the reaction you are after. Remember mankind is basic. Whilst I'm not saying you should deviate from what makes you feel comfortable, it is almost not worth sending this sort of message to your partner. This is romantically worded with a hint of sex and men would prefer, well, sex to be honest.

The problem is of course two-fold. You will be afraid that any message you send might be shown to other people, though as I said in my experience this never happens. More fundamentally is the whole subject of "dirty talk" itself and how open you can be, how open you want to be. I cannot at all advocate anything you don't feel comfortable with but I can assure you that mankind is perfectly comfortable with dirty talk. They practice it enough with their mates, all be it not about you as I covered earlier, but they certainly do. They may not be comfortable in bed saying all sorts of things, but they are when hidden by a phone screen.

So instead of the above message, a man would react better to something like:

"I don't want to be sitting here alone I want to be doing filthy things to you".

In my survey, 92% of men would have preferred the text I write above to the one the columnist suggested in her article.

2) *"If I could wear 3 items of clothes tonight for you what would it be?"*

You don't mean a wool knitted jumper here you mean Lingerie.

This "tease" type of text again is phrased gently in the suggestion by the columnist. It is helpful with a tiny hint of being suggestive but it won't blow your man's mind into a sexual frenzy.

The series of texts with your partner following that opening could well end up like,

"If I could wear 3 items of clothes tonight, what would they be?"

"Err, I like that black skirt you wore the other night"

"That's not what I meant honey"

"What do you mean then aren't we going out?"

"Yes, but I meant for later in the evening"
"When we get home?"

"Yes"

By then of course the moment has gone. The impact has gone.

If you had sent this message *"I can't decide if I should wear a baby doll or be totally naked when we have sex tonight"* you would not have received anything in reply as your husband would already be in the car driving home early, a love-sick puppy under the spell of its master.

3) *"I'm imaging you making love to me by pushing my body against the wall"*
This one is half right.

The problem here are the words *"making love"* which men simply don't say at all. They say "sex" or "fuck". Sorry but they do. It doesn't mean they don't like emotional romantic sex it's just their brain doesn't start with that thought. Here, the impact of *"against the wall"* has been softened by the *"making love"* part and let's face it, if you are pushed against the wall, you are likely to be passionately "fucking" not "making love" in that softer sense.

As a childishly helpful summary, these are the type of sex texts that would work for mankind:

1) *I'm looking through your Instagram photos and touching myself. I hope that's okay.*

2) *I'm completely naked right now getting ready, except for my high heels.*

3) I wish you were in bed with me instead of this vibrator.

and if you are really brave and only if you are comfortable with this sort of thing then try

4) If it takes me a while to answer your texts tonight, it's because I'm watching porn.

The digital explosion has also brought into our vocabulary a new language - the emoji. There are 3,019 of them apparently and women are 36% more likely to use them than a man. A man's emoji range has a smiley face, a love heart, a sad face and maybe one random one that he thought was funny at the time, something like the middle finger one he could send to a friend.

The problem with emojis for mankind is therefore considerable, not in their use but in the understanding of what they actually are. The dangers lurk everywhere, I know one man who received an emoji from a lady at his work, a "nose" and she had added "*this needs to be blowed*" as she had the flu. He read the nose emoji as meaning a knob (as it looks like that, with two nostrils at the bottom mistaken for two balls) and so replied with what he wanted to do sexually to her as well. Lucky for him she had a sense of humour.

Digital communication has also taken over the way we deal with things after a break up. The posting of pictures on say Instagram is a very powerful weapon in a lady's armoury if a man has left her. I will cover this in the break up section but a picture of you looking happy, lovely, laughing, pretty much immediately the break up happens is communication guaranteed to send shock waves into his new grass is greener world.

Alternatively, ladies can use things like hashtags to make their point if a man has left her. The best way to communicate to a man is subtly though because a #fuckyou is just resentment and anger and even more reason for him to then give you the same back. It's the hint of *great I am free at last* (even if that is the last thing on your mind then) which will hurt his pride, and shake the *PANDER* values to its very core.

Things like

#thankyounext

But when you reflect upon society today, communication in a marriage is so vital and yet we are happy to subcontract that out to a piece of technology we hold in our hand. However, it is only non-digital communication which will show all the emotions both of you need to have a healthy relationship.

This can be done in numerous ways large or small. If he is sitting watching something on TV, come up behind him, just touch his shoulders and then smile as you walk by. Enough said. Just stare at him sometimes and when he asks why say *"because I love looking at you"*. At a dinner party just walk past him casually, touch his bum and walk on.

Just that simple gesture says it all in one go and feeds all the *PANDER* values he has.

Annual review

Having thought this whole thing through in some depth I am going to propose something quite radical to you.

When we first meet our partner, we naturally are inquisitive, we ask questions, we are interested, we learn about each other and it's then that any sort of foundation is formed or not. But after a while we stop learning because we become lazy, we become settled. We often don't want to confront problems because it may hurt us to hear about the faults and failures which we are bound to have as the years march on.

However, understanding and knowing each other's points of views, knowing how your partner likes or dislikes things, agreeing on your goals moving forward, all those things are vital. At work there will be communication on everything, you will have a yearly appraisal, you discuss what you like and don't like about the job with colleagues every day. At school you get a report each year on your child, you get a parents evening to discuss things and this is accepted as a normal process.

You will get appliances serviced every year to check they are OK, your car has an MOT to see if it is still roadworthy. You will practice your hobbies, sports, cooking, whatever and you will learn new ways and skills over the years to improve things.

Throughout your life, "new knowledge" is vital and you will gladly take on that quest to look for it.

But you never do that formally in your relationship ever.

In everyday life outside your relationship there are plans for future years. Your company will have short term, medium- and long-term goals set, we elect MP's based upon what they plan to do for the next 5 years, we plan ahead for our children's education.

Yet we never set relationship 5-year goals, 10-year etc. goals formally ever.

The most important thing in your life and you never review it in detail. You gain your knowledge of the partner you have sitting 5 meters away from you by looking at his social media. Feelings, wants, hobbies, sexual fantasies, career goals, anything that affects you change all the time as you get older and yet we never process that properly between partners.

I am therefore advocating an annual review to be done by both of you. It's not romantic but it's essential. The upside far outweighs the downside of a row you may have following it and once you are through one, each year after that becomes easier. It would cover things like your finances, your highs and lows of the years, your current hobbies, your sex life.

Go away for the night and over dinner discuss the annual review. Go back to the place maybe where you had your first date. You will be astonished to see how healthy that process actually is. It will help to stop problems before they arise, it will save marriages, it will make the time with your partner more productive, more focused and you will understand each other far better.

That is communication.

5 HIS BEST FRIEND

I wanted to make this the first chapter but it's a topic we needed to be friends first before I could unleash upon you the subject of all subjects. This isn't intellectual stuff you are about to read, it is shallow, it is stereotypical, but it is absolutely vital nonetheless in your journey to uncover mankind's holy grail.

A man's best friend according to the cliché is, apparently, a dog. You can understand why.

A dog will perform 5 of the 6 *PANDER* values, so it's an obvious match made in pander heaven. Respect is shown when the dog is taught to sit for its "master", it is always enthusiastically wagging its tail when the man gets in, there is a need to be fed, to be stroked, to be walked and the way the dog sits beside its owner shows how proud it is be associated with him.

But there is another best friend, a friend who he loves and hates in equal measure depending upon the circumstances and one who he simply cannot live without in his life. It is a friend who is central to mankind's thinking and embraces all of his *PANDER* values in one go.

You?

I'm afraid not.

It's his knob.

But unlike a normal friendship a man has 4 major issues with it. Actually, make that 5 if you consider that most of the time he acts like a complete and utter cock.

They are, in no order or importance

- losing his erection with a lady or indeed not even getting one at all.
- Cumming too quickly.
- Not Cumming with enough, well, cum.
- How big his cock actually is.

Erection

Now we are really getting to the very soul of breaking the man's secret code here.

The erection is an eternal problem for mankind, something that shows their true deep-rooted vulnerability because "humiliation" can arrive in a 10 second disaster if his best friend decides to not come out and play. I therefore appeal to your kind nature and sense of fairness on this subject, which I know is unlikely, but I urge you at least to try before you laugh your head off at what you are about to read.

There are apparently 18 reasons why a man could lose an erection, ranging from health issues to nervousness. I would actually add one more to that list making it 19 because sometimes it just happens for no reason whatsoever. To make matters worse, a man often has 3-5 erections in his sleep as his nervous system is more active when his eyes are shut. There is therefore no logic to it at all. He may be dreaming of little bunny rabbits hopping around the garden on a summers evening with a huge hard on at that very thought, yet he couldn't get an erection 2 hours previously despite the fact you were lying naked next to him with your hand on his balls.

Within those 18 reasons, not once does it mention *"because he didn't fancy the women"*. And that is 1,000% true. A man losing his erection is not a women's fault, not a reflection on her, not anything she has done wrong. I appreciate that is a hard concept to grasp but it's totally true.

When that erection goes both parties are between a rock and a hard place. Or, in fact, a soft place if you want to be all technical about it. The automatic reaction for a lady then is one of two things. She will probably show her usual caring side, *"don't worry, I'm sure it will be ok"* but that will just make the man feel even more worthless. If a woman instead try's the sexual route with, *"I will get it back up again baby don't you worry"* it is actually the last thing he wants right then as his cock has probably shrunk into near invisibility and if you have trouble even finding it, it won't help his confidence at the very moment his complete and utter downfall has arrived.

This risk and huge doubt over the performance of a man's best friend is almost certainly why there are currently 298 different vibrators and dildos on sale for women at Ann Summers. 42% of women between the ages of 35 to 55 have at least 5 sex toys. That tells you all you need to know and exactly what competition mankind is up against. It doesn't matter how much alcohol you put in it, doesn't matter what sort of day it has had, let's face it 4 AA batteries and a *Rampant Rabbit vibrator* won't ever let you down.

Losing an erection with a girl is therefore the height of mankind's embarrassment. The person you are with thinks he is Zeus but in one act of huge cock betrayal, he becomes *little knob Bob.*

Sex is the greatest physical act mankind will do. Yet with all the other physical acts he gets involved with, he will more often than not do a warm up in preparation like he does in a football game or when he goes for a run. But not in this case. How can he warm up to get his cock warmed up? A quick pull of it to get it interested again? He will definitely try.

The problem is at its highest when you first meet him and the time has arrived to have sex. He will be nervous and any slight feeling of butterflies, then there is a strong possibility his knob isn't going anywhere northwards quickly. Your man could be as sexually excited as he has ever been, be more attracted to you than any women he has ever laid eyes on, but all that will mean nothing to his cock when he feels under pressure.

Those nerves will sweep through his body heading downwards towards his most cherished and important asset. It has become a self-fulfilling prophecy as his brain has talked his cock into something it wasn't planning to do in the first place.

If you have especially just first met, when you are getting ready for the night time action in the bathroom, he isn't getting the candles ready in *le boudoir* and pouring champagne for you, oh no, he is wanking his knob like a madman to get it hard.

I heard of a bloke who slapped it to make sure it went up. Yep, you heard that right. Imagine walking in on that when you are about to have sex for the first time. You are wearing a sexy baby doll with lots of perfume and there he is standing up, whacking his knob like John Cleese did with that branch on the car in Fawlty Towers.

In porn movies they actually have someone called a fluffer to make sure the male porn stars stay hard, with pre sex sex. Now that job wouldn't get advertised in the employment section of the Guardian let me tell you. And next time you talk about fluffing the pillows or the cushions that will take on a whole new meaning.

However, a saviour has now arrived for mankind, the greatest thing to happen in their world since someone thought to roll a pig skin into a circle shape and call it a football. This miracle was small in size yet massive in physical effect and it is now man's new best friend, his protector, his instant confidence boost, the love of his life and the one thing he can't do without.

I regret to say that Homosapien's new wonder lust isn't you once again.

Its's Viagra

And what a knight in shining armour it was. Initially designed for the older gentleman, or those with a genuine medical issue, it quickly turned into a blue pill popping free for all. Men became junkies and were very proud to be. It arrived onto the market in 1988 and in those early days, you had to know someone who could get them for you, forcing cocaine sellers to turn into Viagra dealers which was ironic as cocaine makes mankind lose an erection anyway.

In today's world though they are very easy to get hold of online. A man completes a questionnaire, lying in every answer he gives to every medical question that comes his way and voila £60 gets you 8 pills which when bitten in half, effectively gives 16 erections. That's £3.75 per sexual encounter and therefore the greatest value of all time in his world, cheaper than a pint of lager and a monthly subscription to Sky Sports.

84% of men aged 25+ have apparently taken a Viagra at one point in their lives, which means they will then have taken it multiple times as you are hooked from the first swallow. It is the most addictive chemical in society because it allows a man to be a man. Don't be offended whatsoever if your man takes one, it is not a reflection at all on how turned on he is by you, it's simply an insurance policy for his ego.

What is surprising about it, bearing in mind men don't talk to friends about sex with their partners pretty much ever, the discussion of Viagra is actually not uncommon. It's mankind bonding at its finest, a feeling that we are all in it together and therefore there is no shame attached to asking if anyone has one as you leave the pub that night.

So, how can you tell if he has taken one?

Well, you might see him shove one into his gob in front of you which would in fairness be a bit of a give-away but if he doesn't tell you, then there are some warning signs to watch out for. His chest will start to go a bit red after 15 minutes and he will sound a bit bunged up. He would usually take it 45 minutes before sex, so if you are leaving a restaurant watch what he does. If he fiddles in his pocket, he isn't looking for change to leave as a tip, he is searching for the blue pill he put in there 2 hours previously.

There are massive side effects with taking a Viagra though which rise if you take a whole pill rather than bite one into two. When sex is over and you snuggle up in bed falling asleep in a post sexually relaxed high, content that all seems well in your life and your relationship, he is lying there next to you with chest pains, a rash on his chest glowing like the summer sun, a headache from the depths of hell and not a hint of saliva anywhere in a mouth that now resembles the Sahara Desert in August.

That's new romance for you right there.

How big his cock is

This is serious business now. A man can be defined by this and there isn't much he can do about it. It's a source of ridicule, no scrap that it's the number one source of ridicule if a lady wants to insult a man.

As I am about to set out the physiological effect of this dilemma on mankind I am now seriously breaking mankind's secret code, the oath of allegiance to his fellow comrades. I am turning super grass and laying bare the insecurity's that sit within a man about his best friend.

The average size of a man's knob is 5.3 inches apparently. The average size of a man you will see in a porn film is 9.4 inches. The fantasy ladies is therefore always going to be better than the reality.

It is at this point you need to distinguish between a non-erect knob and one that is hard. There is a massive difference. Literally sometimes. A non-erect penis's average size is about 2.5 inches but quite often it can be less than that, but still grow to a good size.

So, when you throw out the "small cock" insult are you talking erect or non-erect? He may be say 2 inches soft (below average) but that then can grow to say 6.5 inches hard (above average). So, has he a small cock or not by definition? I think it is important to be technically correct before launching any knob abuse but somehow, I don't think you will be considering this vital point as you shout *"tiny todger tosser"* at him for cheating on you.

It is a badge of honour to a man if he has a large penis and his friends will definitely know about it if he does. Hints are dropped in conversation and we are certainly all jealous at that point. We may pretend otherwise but we are. But it stops there, no one actually asks to see it and whilst he may, after several pints, slap it out on the table for some laughs, he would never get it hard first and shout "look at this lads".

His knob has a partner attached it which is the other mankind bollocks. The real bollocks not the bollocks bollocks that comes out of his mouth. Apparently, men touch their balls on average 7 times a day, according to a survey of 2,000 of them carried out in America. Why anyone surveyed this at all is beyond me but it opens the door to a few interesting observations nonetheless.

A few of the reasons for my sensational ball touching revelation is that apparently, he may be adjusting himself if his underwear is too tight or it could just be he is warming his cold hands and the groin area is one of the bodies hotspots. None of the survey participants however confessed that the ball touching was a "ruse" solely to check if the size of his knob had grown any more overnight.

But you can't rule that possibility out comrades.

A penis hard is a penis hard, in that the size doesn't change but a soft cock has a general range of at least an inch and a half which is vital in mankind's insecure mindset. It can happen in cold weather, which makes a penis much smaller apparently because the body is trying to protect it from the temperature. Now as much as I'm sure mankind appreciates this very generous attempt by its body to help him out, he would much prefer it if that protection mechanism buggered off and left his prized possession at a reasonable length in case he got lucky that night.

That survey also conjures up the imagine of multiple germs on his hands 7 times a day. The next time your partner lovingly holds your hand in the movies forget the romance, you better be off to the toilets quick sharp in the movie's quiet bit for a good wash.

The final piece of mankind bollocks enlightenment for your reading pleasure is this. The balls are a very, very sensitive part of his body. This explains the heightened sexual enjoyment he gets when they are touched by his partner or indeed licked or stroked with say satin or silk but to the other extreme it also explains why it downright bloody hurts if they are "knocked" in any way or if a ball hits them there during a sports match.

Now I'm not advocating violence in any shape or form ever but if you find out he has cheated on you, don't slap him round the face in a display of your hurt and anger, kick him in the nuts before you storm out which will get you much closer to the revenge you are after as he doubles up in severe pain and falls to the floor in guilt ridden agony.

In the course of writing this book I discussed with a girlfriend the subject of a mans knob. She immediately asked what we thought about the size of their vagina. Which stunned me I have to say. She told me she had a friend who went to Turkey to get it "tightened" but I have never once, in all my years, meeting thousands of men discussed or heard being discussed the size of the gap of a women's vagina. And in my survey, only 8% said they ever thought about it.

A man will measure the size of his cock regularly and the decimal point strategy to him is vital, though he will be economical with the truth. If it measures 6.2 inches, he will say 6.2 inches but if it is 6.51, he will say it is 7 inches. It is called *bloke rounding* and is officially recognised in all man caves across the world as simple basic mathematics all be it the kind they don't teach you in school.

He will also know that you look at the bulge in his trousers. Come on admit it you do. And I can assure that most men, at some point in their lives, would have put a sock down there before he went out to make up for any visual "shortfalls".

So, assuming a male gets through the first hurdle of actually being able to get his cock up, then he has the next problem, which is essentially, should he have even bothered to in the first place.

It is at this point though I want to stand up for mankind rather than ridicule them as I often do in this book. We are born with what we are born with. It is what it is and yet throughout our whole lives we are defined as either "quantity not quality" or "quality not quantity" depending on the size of the knob we were given at birth. But think about this. If you stay with your partner in the longer term then effectively you knew what you had gotten yourself into when you first slept with him.

It's sold as seen I'm afraid.

If you go into a garage and buy a mini it won't ever turn into an articulated lorry. A man cannot increase the size of it, there is basically nothing major he can do to change what he has been gifted by his parents. There are some things for sale like a penis vacuum pump but it's hardly the most romantic thing in the world you laying there naked on silk sheets, sipping champagne and him next to you with a small hover around his cock trying to inflate the prized possession.

To further "educate" you on the biggest, or indeed smallest issue, in mankind's brain go into google now and type in "small penis humiliation" (SPH). There are 14 million entries. This is not what you think at first sight, which is page after page of ladies shaming men they know, it is in fact a fetish fantasy that mankind themselves desire.

To be humiliated for having a small penis and they then get sexually aroused from that. It is *PANDER* reversal and that apparently can stimulate a chemical that excites a man. Because to the outside world they are so "powerful" yet actually want to be humiliated behind the scenes.

Men therefore pay adult workers, either to see them in person or on the phone or via webcam to give them SPH. There are hundreds of words for a small cock apparently which will be shouted at you. There are 14 hand gestures that can be made. There are over 200,000 clips on Pornhub, the biggest porn site in the world on that very subject. It is out there, and I will be scared for life for researching it I'm sure, having seen a few of these clips to make sure I wasn't dreaming it.

Back in the real world, men do not take the micky out of other men for having "a small cock". I've never heard one man say that to anyone, which may because we don't disclose. the sizes of our cocks, unless it's large. But it's not used as a generic insult either. This may be an unsaid man code of honour who knows but it is a fact nonetheless.

A question I have been asked again and again bizarrely when writing this book was not about love or romance or valentine's day it was *"do men look at other men's knobs when they are stood next to each other in a urinal to see how big they are"*. And it's a fair question when you think about it.

The quick answer is no they don't there is once again a man's code not to do that or indeed even to chat to each other when they are stood side by side.

A lady's toilet is as it should be, your private space behind a locked door for a moment of privacy. A man's toilet is simply another world.

There is usually only one private cubicle, and if it's in a pub, racetrack, football match, concert or anything like that, that cubicle has a huge queue of people waiting to use it. This has nothing to do with what you think a man would want privacy for at that moment, oh no my friends, it is solely because they want to do a line of cocaine in secret. It is an utterly hilarious sight. Grown men lined up, not looking at each other, trying to act innocently, staring at their phone but all with a restless twitch about them which miraculously disappears when they walk out of the cubicle smiling and sniffing merrily away.

To prove the point about men not looking at the size of another man's penis in the toilets, I offer up this shameful story as a case for the defense. I have been fortunate to have met many "A list" celebrities in my life which included having lunch with Gary Barlow and a visit to see Robbie Williams in his hotel suite aka *the two Take That famous ones*.

I don't know why though but Howard from Take That was the person I only ever wanted to meet. Absolutely no idea why. So much so that my phone's name was "Howard" until I discovered one day someone trying to Bluetooth me something in a really important meeting and asking whose phone was "*Howard*"?

"*No idea mate*".

But eventually I did meet him, just the once. Not sure you could call it a proper meeting but a meeting it was in my definition none the less. I walked into Zuma restaurant in Mayfair and there he was by the bar with a girl. I was about to walk over and introduce myself, as you do, but then I thought hang on this looks like a first date between them he is not going to be happy and I don't want to ruin my one chance.

He sat down to eat very close to where we were and I worked out the strategy. I would wait until he went to the toilet and I would follow him in. A genius plan except he wasn't drinking, he was sipping water.

I wasn't drinking water, I was sipping wine. OK Gulping wine actually. An hour I waited, legs crossed getting desperate so I re-evaluated the strategic plan.

1) I could wet myself there and then at the table but I did still have 5% of my dignity intact. Though my wife at that time would have no doubt taken issue with that.

2) I could run to the toilet now, go quickly, then hover generally outside the toilet door until he arrived. But Zuma is well known for the Russian mafia and one was selfishly bound to go to the toilet at some point. Even though I would intellectually try and argue with their bodyguards, previously in the SAS, that "*no honestly I'm waiting to hang out with Howard from Take That in the toilets?*", being part of the Iranian siege of 1980 and thus by definition proper hard men, they may not believe me before they karate kicked me in the nuts.

3) I could start liking Mark Owen from Take That instead. In a shallow traitor sort of way. But it's like a football team, you must support forever who you started to support as a youngster and its bad Karma to change.

But then like a miracle not seen since biblical times 2,000 years before, he got up from his seat. I jumped up and followed him, two steps behind. In fairness, it may have been one step but I'm trying to sound like I wasn't a stalker in that moment. I started to walk cool, but unfortunately, I had that look of agony that follows you when you are dying for a piss.

So not acting cool at all, I followed him in my mind strutting like John Travolta in Saturday Night Fever but instead walking like a chicken who needed a piss.

We virtually went into the toilet together and there it was. Two urinals, separated by a small glass privacy divider. He took the far one, I wasn't going to argue with him. He was a rock star.

And there we were both were, side by side.

Now at this point we need to get a perspective on this. I'm next to my hero. I'm dying to go to the toilet and he probably isn't, the health freak. What do I do? It isn't sociable to lean over and try and shake his hand as he is going. Or indeed peer over and look at his knob as I mentioned before. And I really hoped he wouldn't peer over and look at my knob either. Don't judge me. It had been an unusually cold night out there.

And so it was total silence staring at the wall ahead until we reached the sinks at which time I rest my case, your honour, even in moments of hero worship, men don't break the "look at each others knob" code.

So, having given you a deeper understanding on the sensitivities surrounding the size of his knob, let us test your newly found "compassion" on the subject.

A friend told me a story once of a first date he had which went well enough to move to stage 2 very quickly. Back at the hotel bedroom with her that night, the "action" started and he went behind her in the doggy position, thrusting away thinking what an incredible first date this had become. That feeling lasted approximately one minute because as he got into his rhythm, the lady he was with turned her head around and uttered the worse combination of words mankind can ever hear

"I can't feel anything babe, it's not in yet, is it?"

Compassionate?

Nope. You are laughing now aren't you.

Philistines.

Lack of Cum from a man

When you watch a porn film, which you will deny you ever have but secretly do, the man you see on screen is not like 99.99999% of the rest of the male population throughout the world.

He has a great body, a big and thick cock, can last for hours and when he cums it gushes out like a volcanic spurt of white fire enough to cover Pompeii itself 2,000 years previously. You never see an overweight, small cock, slightly drunk man who cums within 4 minutes, spurting out a little dribble at the end when his orgasmic conclusion arrives.

Women have the upper hand here. When they cum, it isn't visible. You might say you are cumming in that moment but it isn't external as such. A man leaves evidence of his "enjoyment" and it's another pressure moment for him. But the amount of sperm can often not equate at all to the experience he has had. It is simply not connected. It is in the lap of the cock Gods and once again, a man is born with the DNA to ejaculate a lot or he isn't.

Not his fault.

For once.

There isn't much a man can do about it. He can apparently try and increase his chances of a "decent" ejaculation through more Vitamin C and D as it helps the amount of sperm that is set free to discover life outside a man's balls but that's about all. So, it is fair to conclude that when you see your man suddenly eating oranges and egg yolk on a Friday afternoon, it is not for fitness reasons it's to try and get more than a teaspoon of cum ready for that evening, when his encore moment arrives.

He is considerate and kind like that.

A man will rarely, in fact borderline never, discuss this issue with their friends though.

I only know of one instance where I have heard this being talked about by a man, who reckoned he *came* so much he could hit the ceiling with it. He seemed pretty confident of that fact, though none of us in the room at that time asked him to prove it, we didn't want to see him wanking off on the floor as we watched the football. That could be a bad thing though for a lady if true. If you don't like the taste of sperm, half a carton of cream poured down your throat is not going to help the situation.

Finally, a word of warning on this dilemma, a dilemma you didn't know you had until I mentioned it. If your man is a *"super spunker"* then be warned. You may be lying in bed one night, dozing off, when you feel a drip drip onto your head.

Don't panic.

It may not be a leak from the water pipes above, it could well that your man had just had a play and it is now all just dripping onto your head.

Cumming too quickly

During sex, women can often have multiple orgasms. When a man cums, that is usually it for a while. Or indeed that is that for the next few days as he gets older. During ejaculation, men release (wait for it) a cocktail of brain chemicals, including norepinephrine, serotonin, oxytocin, vasopressin, nitric oxide and last but not least the hormone prolactin.

That's a lot of chemicals to get out of your system. It is therefore a supreme "de-arouser" when he cums and temporarily decreases his desire for sex. Instantly. As a woman feels more emotionally attached to her partner after sex, a man only feels emotionally attached to the TV remote control, so he can lay back and watch Match of the Day.

It's not just the lack of action after he has cum that may be a problem. If a lady hasn't orgasmed at that moment, then her chances of getting her man to do that for her will be slim. There is no encore. It's a bit like if you were at a Robbie Williams concert and he pisses off just as you are getting ready for the grand finale

"*Oi Robbie where's Angels?*" the crowd shouts

"*Sorry, I've cum, that's the end of the show*".

You may want your money back.

And if all that wasn't bad enough, we have mankind's problem of cumming too quickly and he will try anything to stop that happening. Personally, and without saying which women this may have related too (though probably all at some stage in fairness), I used to think of cold toast to keep me from cumming too early when I had sex. And if I was really turned on my thoughts would be cold toast and marmite. If I was really really turned on, I would sing a song right the way through instead in my head and if I was

particularly impressive that night, on those very rare occasions, I would need to sing it again and again.

And most of the time for me that song would be *Let's Dance* by David Bowie. Now that's a secret revealed right there for what its' worth to no-one probably.

"*God you are so hard baby it feels sooooooo great*" she would purr to me

"*Put on your red shoes and dance the blues?*" I would purr to myself in my head

"*You are so wonderful*" she would cry out to no one listening, in huge admiration

"*Under the moonlight, the serrrrrious moonlight*" I would silently sing to myself thrusting harder at the last part to keep in tune with the beat

And sometimes in extreme circumstances, my friends, I would imagine Bowie eating cold toast and marmite singing Let's Dance. Always worked for me.

So, ladies when he is having sex with you tonight, I'm sorry but the chances are he isn't thinking lovely things about you, he is simply singing YMCA to himself.

6 JEALOUSY

If you really love someone, you will at times get jealous.

It is a natural human reaction which could cover many areas of life, but relationships in particular. It is *"good jealousy"*. Why wouldn't you occasionally have that fear of losing something you love. That type of emotion is rational, it is dealt with, it is communicated and it is discussed.

However, the words *"you are jealous"*, makes it sound like you are obsessive, controlling and somewhat weird but every single person on this earth will have been jealous for some reason at some point in their lives.

If you suspect your partner of cheating, for example, of course you will develop jealousy. If you just sat there and didn't care then you simply do not love the person you are in a relationship with. A healthy jealousy from a woman is welcomed by mankind. That shows love, shows feelings, shows you care. He won't think you are some psycho stalker he will feel a lot of the *PANDER* values right at that moment.

But as with most things regarding your relationship, communication is key.

If, for example, you look over at a party and another lady is talking to your man and starts touching his arm as he talks to her, he may be oblivious to that but you know it's flirting and quite rightly you may feel those healthy jealous butterflies inside of you. And say in this case, you tell your man when you get home you weren't comfortable with what you saw, he should respect that, apologise for it and ensure he is aware of it going forward,

However, say the in the above case the positions were reversed and it was a man who was putting an arm on you as your husband watched from afar. There is a strong chance he would confront that 3rd party there and then and blow it all out of all proportion. It's the feeling his *PANDER* values have been tainted. Even worse though is that one event could start the trigger to unhealthy jealousy.

Good and bad jealousy sit on a rocky tightrope as there is often a fine line between acceptable normal feelings and possessiveness. When it steps over that mark to the dark side, the whole thing is a totally different ball game.

Bad jealousy is potentially a very harmful thing in your relationship. If you have it, your mind plays tricks on you. It kills you inside, it takes control of you. It is the snake of all emotions and its venom will give you death by a thousand cuts. The worse part of unhealthy jealousy is the unknown. If you knew the truth you could at least deal with it and after a break up especially it can get worse, you want closure but you often don't get it.

Jealousy at its core is a by-product of fear, fear of not being good enough, the fear of loss. When it hits, it can trick us into believing our relationship is in immediate danger, making it impossible to distinguish between normal and strange things. Paranoid suspicion takes over.

In other words, it is simply fucking terrible.

Bad jealousy can easily start to then turn abusive. If you have a very jealous man, then he may start trying to control many parts of your life initiating a chain of events that makes your everyday existence hell on earth.

A healthy relationship of course involves time apart it simply has to. You need space and a man does to. But if your man starts to ask you to ditch your friends or turn up uninvited when you are with them then this is not good at all. Whilst it may seem sweet that he wants to spend all of his time with you, a person with respect will understand that you need time away from the relationship.

And you deserve time to be alone and pursue other interests without facing "punishment" for it.

Communication is absolutely vital if you recognise *bad jealousy* in your man and it has to be dealt with at the earliest stage possible. If you believe you are in a healthy relationship but your man has *bad jealousy* then all is not lost, the whole thing can be dealt with. In some ways this type of feeling in your man is an early form of addiction, because something has triggered it. This addiction is you and he is terrified of it being taken away from him.

Any form of "addiction" should not be met with anger, insults or disdain it should be faced head on with understanding and compassion. If you are married remember it is *for better for worse in sickness and in health*. Of course, if it becomes intolerable after trying to help then you have to make a conscious decision in your best interests but if you want to still be with him then it needs to be tackled sensitively.

A man has *bad jealousy* because he will feel his *PANDER* values are under attack. He will feel he isn't desired by you as much, that you are showing no respect to him, that you may need someone else more than him. This may be totally irrational and often it is but you need to understand why and then deal with it with empathy.

You should sit him down and ask calmly why he feels as he does and what you have done to trigger that within him. This should be followed up by asking what you can do to prove he has no need to be jealous in the short term. Research shows that someone's routine and brain will switch into a new pattern after 21 days and so you may have to compromise your normal way of doing things, your normal social pattern, over 3 weeks to help this part of your relationship.

A mental issue, which jealousy is of sorts, needs healing and fixing. If your man had a physical injury, he may have surgery and you would no doubt understand and compromise your routine for that because it is something visual you can react to. The problem with mental health is that it is hidden and so we don't relate to it the same way. We don't treat it with the same concern and respect we do to anything physically wrong with us.

So, having communicated and calmly discussed things with him, you will need action on top of words. This may involve for a few weeks, being more attentive to him if you go out with your friends. Text him more regularity to reassure him. Increase your *PANDER* actions to him in numerous ways. Shouting at him "*you are being ridiculous*" won't stop the growth of bad jealousy but if you are willing to understand and show that you love him by compromising then it is highly likely you will back to a solid relationship once again and the *bad jealousy* will ease.

However.

If after being patient, understanding, giving actions not words in the short term to try and help the issue, it keeps repeating and repeating for no logical reason then it may start to turn into genuine domestic abuse. Domestic abuse can occur in non -jealous people but it is more likely if you are in a possessive/bad jealousy relationship.

Any form of proven abuse in modern day society is disgusting. No one should be a shadow of themselves and that is what it does to you if you are a victim.

Violent abuse is much easier to spot because there will likely be evidence of say a "mark" on the face, an injury, friends would spot something. It may be so bad that an instant call to the police is made. Domestic abuse, its evil partner, the archetypal Bond Villain, is much harder to prove and to spot because by its very nature it happens over a period of time.

Men are more likely to cause domestic abuse than women according to studies. The ratio is 75-25, but the ratio of violent abuse is 60-40 men to women.

Domestic abuse has now effectively been renamed *Coercive Control*. That term was born from the aftermath of the #metoo campaign which started after the Weinstein affair. The police in this country are taking any claim of alleged *Coercive Control* (CC) very seriously.

At a high level, CC will exist if your man tries to influence who you can speak to, if they monitor you online constantly and berate you for who you are interacting with. It will be there if they try and dictate your day to you, limiting the time you spend with others. It happens if your man tells you what you should wear each day, if he undermines you constantly both publicly and privately, if he constantly shouts at you, accuses you of all sorts of things, continually trying to put you down at home or in front of other people.

Someone who is domestically abusing you may also try and regularly control your finances, prevent you from working properly, almost delight in the joy of making you beg for money. And CC could then move to violent abuse, punching, kicking, slapping, pinching, burning, pinning you down if you don't let your partner "control" you domestically.

Let me make this absolutely clear. If you are being domestically or violently abused then leave your relationship. Do not compromise, do not stay for the sake of the children, do not accept what is being done to you.

The only reason to consider returning is if it is shown your partner has a mental issue, such as Borderline Personality Disorder, which can be treated and would explain why the abuse was happening at least. However, other personality disorders such as Narcissistic Personality Disorder cannot be treated and you should run as quickly as you can getting help from your friends and family and the authorities as you do.

Having said that, be sure about CC. Not every bad thing is that. Everyone will row at some point and say nasty things they almost certainly do not mean. Sometimes your man is a complete arse which shows he is just an idiot it doesn't mean he is controlling you.

There is a fine line but it is a clear fine line. Domestic abuse will happen over time, violent abuse is something which happens immediately. It is important to apply common sense to every situation, to conclude if a pattern is developing because an accusation of CC is a serious offence and could get out of hand quickly, especially if you are in the throes of a divorce where claim and counter claim will be flying around.

Some examples of how to tell if your man is Coercive Controlling you

Nights out
A man is a "protector" and so it's natural that he wants to make sure his partner is safe. For example, if you are away for the night, it's not wrong for him to ask for a quick text at some point to see if you are OK and having fun. It is not wrong as a consequence for him to get worked up a bit if you don't do that or forget to.

But if he demands constant attention even though you are out with your friends, texting you every half hour or even following you then that is not a good sign. If he does that consistently, making you not want to socialise in the future with anyone but him, then that is a sign of control.

It has to be judged in perspective. Say you have cheated on him in the past and he reasonably asks in the short term, whilst you rebuild trust, to "check in" more, maybe doing a video call to prove where you are, then that isn't unhealthy jealousy it is reasonable in the circumstances.

Finances
By its very nature, if the man for whatever reason is the main earner in the family, then he is controlling money. Track back 30 years before society finally woke up, this was part of the stereotypical mankind v women role.

If a man is the bread winner still and a budget is done for the month with say you getting £300 to spend, then as long as that is equal to the man's share, it is reasonable, it is economics it isn't controlling. If that is cut to £100 to spend because of, say, redundancy that isn't CC it is total common sense in that moment.

However, if you have to constantly ask him for money and there is no "budget" system then that maybe is controlling because he will have the power to stop you going out with your friends for example. That is of course totally unreasonable.

What you wear and your appearance in general
It is natural for partners to have views on the things we wear. It is nice if your partner says to you, "*you look so amazing in that, why don't you wear it tonight.*"

But if your man lays out your clothes every day and tells you what to wear constantly then that is controlling. If he is in charge of what style you have, returning things to shops constantly that didn't fit within his criteria then that would also be CC. Having a row about overspending, resulting in something being sent back to a shop on one or two occasions over a number of years isn't.

They Monitor Your Communications
If you are texting late at night and your man comes into the bedroom resulting in you suspiciously turning your phone over, then if he asks to see your phone it is common sense that is reasonable jealousy

If he demands to see your phone every day then that is not healthy at all, it is an invasion of privacy because everyone has private chats with their friends.

If your partner demands to know at all times the passwords to your phone, email account, Facebook, Snap Chat, Instagram and any other social media app you use then that is unhealthy and that is controlling. If they go through your messages, question you about conversations, delete contacts they don't approve of then that is CC. Wanting your passwords is not about love, it is about dominance and control.

If you believe your partner has been coercively controlling you, then you can report them to the police. You can also as a civil process try and gain a non-molestation order, (NMO), like a restraining order, through the courts.

The burden of proof to get the police to arrest your partner and for you to obtain a NMO is very very low, designed like that to help speed the process up. At that stage a person is very much guilty unless they prove themselves innocent.

The court process is designed to respond quickly to accusations before the facts are heard to ensure the safety of the accuser. As such not much, if indeed any, evidence is needed for a NMO to be granted. A form is completed, which can be done by you or a lawyer, and a private hearing is had within 2 days when a judge will grant the order or not. Your partner isn't aware that is happening and they are then served with the order if it is granted.

An appeal is offered but it can take weeks to be heard. The courts therefore take a draconian and cautious approach to every accusation.

A Non-Molestation Order is normally granted for 6-12 months but can be extended for a longer period under specific circumstances. At that stage it is a civil matter and your partner will be precluded from contacting you, to come to the house, or to threaten you or your friends. As long as they don't break those terms it is not a criminal act but if they do then the police can arrest them.

However, whilst the process should be applauded for genuine cases, it is fair to point out a NMO application can be misused and I have known some men who have had that done to them. According to *SAVE* (Stop Abusive and Violent Environments), 10% of the people arrested for domestic abuse are wrongly accused. That in itself is therefore abuse became a false accusation could ruin a person's life.

The reason for a false application is threefold. Under the legal aid rules, divorce costs are not allowed to be claimed unless there is an allegation of domestic abuse. It is therefore a motive at least for a false claim. In a very turbulent marriage, where for example a man has cheated on his partner, it is an obvious form of revenge. It can be used to make access to the children difficult or to get the upper hand in a custody battle.

It is common in people who have personality disorders because they are great liars and have frank regard for the truth at the best of times.

After saying all that, remember though to embrace good jealousy, it means you are in love.

But make sure the communication around it is sensible, it is speedy and it is genuine.

7 CHEATING

Gut feeling.

Does it say he is cheating? Then you may well be right. Studies say that 78% of people who had the sinking feeling their partner was having an affair were correct.

Something is just off and you can't put your finger on it. More often than not the obvious answer is the bleeding obvious. The eternal problem has been of course that we don't want to believe it is true so we try and convince ourselves that the illogical replies to questions we ask our partner must be right, because we do not want to face the reality that isn't just staring us in the face, it is slapping us on the cheeks in a desperate wake up call.

I'm generalising a bit now, as everyone has their own reasons, but the latest surveys published say 25% of men have had an affair and 14% have been with an escort. I cannot make any assumption about woman and how they may cheat, if they do, but study after study highlight that women will rarely cheat for just sexual pleasure, they are more likely to have an emotional attachment to her lover. By inference therefore, women place more "importance" to cheating and it is I am afraid to say, quite often true that men can "cheat" and move on from any guilt very quickly, putting it out of his mind that ever he did just that.

In the case of a one-night stand and an affair, men quite often don't care about "looks". They care about *PANDER*. So of course, if you find out your man has cheated and you quite rightly think "what has she got that I haven't" it might be the case that she simply hasn't got anything you haven't got but what she is doing is either "feeding" his sexual desire (escort, one-night stand) or feeding that fragile ego, in the case of an emotional affair.

Men believe that they will get a second chance if they are "caught out". This is backed up by surveys which say 70% of women would give them that chance, yet 55% of men will still go on to cheat again and only 18% of

marriages survive an affair. The same survey said only 32% of men would give their partner a second chance.

This is the hypocrisy of mankind again. His *PANDER* values make it very difficult for him to accept that his woman has been with someone else and yet those same values make him want to cheat, to get the affirmation he often craves.

This is such a serious point.

Take a look at your partner now, who you love deeply. Look at him. Close your eyes and feel the love you have for him; remember once again all those wonderful times you have spent together.

Now imagine he has had an affair which you have started to suspect and he has left you.

You are reeling, your mind goes back over and over again to the last few months of dark discrepancies which now add up to a brighter shade of reality. You search for some meaning but your only true closure will come from within, the truth is now only the reflection in the mirror you see every day because it is now the only thing you can trust.

Probably for a long time.

The end of this relationship for you will feel like a withdrawal from drug addiction. It will leave you feeling utterly helpless and utterly worthless. Your addiction just cannot be fed anymore. Once you were his heroine, now you are just simply heroin. You want to recapture those early fairy tale months you both had but you can't and the withdrawal pain is simply too much to bear. You are in a dance of defeat and he is setting the rhythm.

You have had doubts for a while. But the high from his drug that you willing injected was always worth the low from the relationship that he gave you. As the end came, so did your need for his approval increase, for any scrap of kindness and any leftovers of sincerity he may give you as you tried to persuade him that the dream he once saw in you was still very much alive. Where you once binged on his affection you now starve from his cruelty. All you will now eat is the crumbs he wants to give you.

Your beauty is destroyed. Memories, happiness, your magic, mean nothing to him now and he has no desire to be reminded of them, he is blinded by the new beautiful vision in his mind of what he believes is the answer. But in your despair, there is no answer for you as he refuses to set the question.

Love is gone. The love of your life has gone. Cupids arrow now has a poisoned tip full of toxic venom which brings you to the very edge of insanity.

The abandonment is like a virus, growing daily, and it has found a willing host to travel through as it makes its way rapidly to your very soul. The fairy tale has now reached midnight and Cinderella must return to where she was before, the illusion of happiness has gone and the glass slipper will never fit again.

He only sees the bad in you, will never acknowledge the good ever again.

You cannot win by persuasion.

At that moment, you cannot win at all.

The danger zone for an affair is in the middle of a relationship, which does make sense when you think about it. But whenever it happens it is clearly the worst thing imaginable in a marriage. On both sides. This book may help stop that happening in some way but you know what, men are so utterly stupid sometimes that even if they had the best relationship they could ever want, some of them will still cheat and not necessarily for sex as we know it to be.

Cheating has evolved into an incredible new arena and the definition we once had of just that, simply is "not that" anymore. Before 1986, the way cheating was defined was purely sexual. But now with the rise of the internet, social media and the mobile phone, a more sinister version of betraying a loved one has arrived into society.

Welcome stage left its twin brothers, emotional cheating and digital cheating.

Sex has always been the definition marker for cheating. But why? Is it now much wider than that now in today's society I am afraid to say.

Ask yourself this

Is Flirting cheating? Flirting is defined as *"behaving in a somewhat amorous or quasi romantic fashion towards someone without intending to be serious"* In other words, being flirtatious does not necessarily mean that someone is trying to become emotionally attached or even attempting to have sex with another person. At the same time, being mildly flirtatious can I suppose be charming.

When does flirting cross over the line into something else? It could be inappropriate touching, inappropriate conversation, giving the signs of a deeper interest e.g. looking into each other's eyes with a slight pause. Depending on the nature of your relationship it may be quite acceptable for either or both of you to be flirtatious with others. This will depend on trust, on communication, on the foundations you have built. But if you don't discuss it at some point, how does anyone know?

Is watching porn without you cheating? Your man is looking at someone else to gain sexual excitement, how far does this cross into an unacceptable boundary? I have no idea what the wrong or right answer is, studies and online chat are divided on this but it is worthy of debate that is for sure. This therefore is something that should be dealt with, confronted and clarified when you know the relationship is going somewhere. We do not like to because it may appear like we are a jealous, controlling, lunatic but it is vital.

How should sex now be viewed as cheating in the modern world today? If he has been with an escort, it may "just" be to gain some sort of sexual experience he was after. That doesn't justify it at all, doesn't make it right in anyway whatsoever but he will never see that girl again and has no interest in her whatsoever when they part company. I don't say that to make it acceptable but to set the scene for this.

When emotional cheating arrives, it is often the cruelest blow because it takes your man's heart with it.

A man won't have emotional cheating with an escort. It is book, pay, act, go. Still utterly wrong but with an affair there is a sustained effort to fool you and a sustained effort to give affection to another person, which should

solely be yours. The phone has caused this version of cheating to explode to almost out of control levels.

Man is driven by sex but if he crosses the boundary to emotional chat in a text well that is not usual for him and therefore that is consciously being different. This isn't man's "animal" instinct anymore; it comes from his heart and not his knob. And if you happened to ever read in a text what someone else is saying to your husband and what he says back, about desire or feelings, then that stuff ruins you for life. You can't unread it.

"I have never felt like this with anyone before in my life" he writes to some other lady.

And you see it. That is cheating. And you would be devastated.

Cheating has also arrived into the digital sex world; the rise of the online sex industry has meant the definition of what could be defined as cheating has changed dramatically.

25 years ago, the way a man saw an escort was to go to a street corner or look in the local paper for an advert. But today it is simply astonishing the sex industry which sits online, what is available and how easy it is to have whatever a man (or women) wants sexually.

This rise of the digital escort is very very worrying for your relationship. Every woman in this country should take a deep breath and look at sites like *"adultwork"* to see what I mean. It is simply jaw dropping and every man I know is aware that site exists as do 94% of the men in the private survey I carried out.

There are 15,000 escorts listed on that site across various areas of the country

London – 4,000

South west – 1,075

Yorkshire – 1,100

North East – 500

Scotland – 1,000

Wales – 500

East midland – 900

Est Anglia – 1,300

North west – 1,700

South east – c1,950

West midlands – c1,200

All of them list the "services" provided and what that will cost. It is like looking at a restaurant's menu, the sexual choice is now as easy as that. If your man has a fetish, he can look down that list, pick the lady he wants and then meet her for £150. Just like that and if say it's on the way home from work, and he meets her at her place (called "incall" which most offer) then there is virtually no way at all you will ever know it happened.

But more worrying is something else on the rise, a new digital led version of a "one-night stand" has arrived into society. With the covid crisis and lockdown, another part of the sex industry rose rapidly in popularity: personalised porn, Webcam shows and audio services. A man can now cheat by opening up his computer and sexually interact with a woman via skype or an adult worker can call him up and basically talk dirty down the phone for as long he wants to them for at £1.50 a minute.

Personalised films can be made by an adult worker. A man requests her to film herself in a certain situation, and pays her for it. They send it to him as a digital file or can actually upload it onto a porn site so he can view it there, without any chance of his partner finding it on his computer. Don't believe me? Look at *"Only fans"* online it's all there in plain view and millions are using it.

Is that cheating? Of course it is. But it is very hard to find out it had happened at all.

Affairs

If a man has an affair, in that now "old fashioned" term, it will either be

1) A casual one, like a work acquaintance on and off with no real intention of him leaving his wife.

2) Because something isn't right between him and his partner and he has found someone else who can reaffirm the *PANDER* he needs, meaning he may actually leave the relationship because of it.

3) Or it is a one-night stand with someone driven entirely by sex.

I have interviewed a lot of men who have cheated, undertaken countless hours of research online and conducted various surveys about all this. Technology has given mankind numerous ways to cheat but it has also given you numerous ways you can catch him at it.

There are now two types of cheaters, and this doesn't give me any joy defining it like this but a man is either a lazy cheater or a professional one.

Catching them starts with the phone.

The lazy cheater

In today's world, the mobile phone holds the key to all life's mysteries. What the phone can reveal to anyone is quite extraordinary, though on the flip side with the development of certain apps it can also cover up a cheater's tracks to an almost impossible level of discovery.

The fast track starting point to catch your man out, without going through any of the other ways I list below and cutting right to the chase, is either you look through his phone if you know his entry code or if you don't know it then you must consider the possibility of demanding to see it, which we will cover later.

Things to consider

- Look for a change of habit with the phone. When you meet someone (and I know this isn't romantic but this is modern day society) one of the first things to do is to memorise how he uses his phones, when he does use it etc. If he is having an affair those patterns will change and you will be able to see those warning signals.

For example

- Does he turn his phone over when he has it with him so you can't see the screen and he never used to? The reason he may do that is the notifications that keep coming will be shown even if its locked. Everyone turns their phone over of course it's a 50-50 chance but watch him and if he constantly does that it could well be a warning sign.

- Is his phone muted in the evenings? Does he protect it as if it is his baby? Does he take it with him everywhere he goes? All warning sings if done constantly.

- If his phone is turned screen up and notifications come through in a general sense like" WhatsApp message" rather than say "Jenny WhatsApp message" then that's a sign that he has consciously turned off the contact details on message notifications.

- Is his phone locked and it never was before? If it never was and now it is then why? Start memorising the number when he types it in, one number at a time when you get the chance to watch him and next time he is drunk or asleep you have a chance to go through it.

If you do get into his phone then what you should do firstly is put your phone behind you on a stand and press record. You need to tape what you see on this phone because this allows you to quickly skim through it. If you are doing it secretly you may not have long. You can then play that recording back later and pause at every bit you want to read properly. As you record his screen go FastTrack through the various places you need to, don't stop and read anything you can do that later. Don't stop, that is vital and don't read it then because if you find one thing suspicious you will be distracted by that and you want all the information that phone is going to reveal.

On an iPhone this is what you need to do

- Go straight to pictures and skim through them but look for the hidden photo albums and in the deleted photos section. Men like to keep "trophies" of their actions.

- Go to contacts because it is likely his affair is under a different name. Skim through each contact and you can check the number later. If you have WhatsApp, you can check the number by putting it into the contacts and a picture of them will turn up if they are on there. If it's a different picture than the contact's name then you are onto something.

- In WhatsApp check linked devices to see if he is using WhatsApp through his laptop. What he may do is pretend to be working at night so you can see he is not on his phone but he is really messaging through his laptop as the phone will Bluetooth the messages to his computer.

- Go to Settings, Notifications and see if he has any social media set for "off" regarding notifications. A cheater will not want a message to show up on screen and with notifications off it will never show up without him going to the app itself.

- Go to Safari and look at the website history. Also go into Settings, Safari, Advanced and there you will see "cookies" stored and they will show sites he has been too if he has already deleted the history section in Safari.

- Go to google maps and see what locations he has searched for or visited.

- Go to his call history and check the timing of calls – it's the first thing and last thing calls you are looking for, even if they seem to be to normal people, these could be the alias.

- Go to screen time and see how long he has spent on various things e.g., Instagram

- If you have his code, go to Settings, Passwords, type the code in and it will come up with all the apps etc he has and what their passwords are. That way you can look at Instagram etc in a more leisurely way because you know the access in. Also, if he used the same passwords everywhere this may then give you access to his emails or anything not on his phone.

- If you then have his password for emails, after you have returned his phone create a new email account on your laptop on outlook, put the password in and you can live track his emails in future and he won't know you are doing it. Outlook does not send a warning that emails are now being shown elsewhere.

- On his Instagram app look at the bottom right of the screen and click it - it will show up any other alias he is using. Look at the searches he has made and of course go into the messages section.

- Go into Settings, notes as he may save old texts there, thinking he was clever deleting them from "messages" itself.

- Sometimes the message isn't there but he has screenshot it to look at through photos. Or he may have an app like photo vault so check the apps he has downloaded.

- Always look at settings, voice memos as he may have tapped interaction e.g. sex

- Look at blocked contacts – he may have blocked them for the time he is with you so they can't suddenly call or message

- WhatsApp can give a code to link to another device, If you scan it you would watch his WhatsApp thorough your computer but this will be shown on his WhatsApp if he goes into settings, linked devices so be careful.

- Look at the pattern of the chat in messages to see if any have been deleted in the middle of a conversation. WhatsApp especially do disappearing messages now.

More "traditional" things to watch out for
1) You are looking for changes in patterns or routines. A man is often set in his ways and so the slightest deviation from that could mean the start of something else. This may be things like spending too

much time in the garden (checking his phone secretly) or re ironing his shirt in the morning when he goes out.

2) Has what he does in bed become different? Has his kissing style changed for example? It is often the case, bizarrely, with an affair you get more sex than usual.

3) Face time him when he is away don't call him and see if he answers.

4) Look at his followers on Instagram, Facebook etc and who is following and who he follows. It's an obvious thing but really study the pattern of who gives likes for example who didn't before. Then look at their pages and see what days posts are made compared to the days you know you were not with your partner. For example, someone revealed to me that they found out their partner was cheating by looking at the Instagram of a make-up artist who started to like his posts. She happened to post a lot of images from around the country and would always give personal details of where she was and every day she said she was in Bristol were the same days her husband was working from home in Bristol.

5) What time is he calling you to say goodnight if he is away on business? An early ish call along the lines of "*I'm tired I an going to bed early*" may be because as he wants the night ahead without you interrupting him. Ring him with a fake emergency an hour later and see if he answers.

6) Is he more shaven than normal when he gets in? Not when he goes out, when he comes in. Compare that to the normal amount of stubble when he gets in because there is only one reason he would be shaving mid-day.

7) Men will want to keep a bag (with aftershave etc) or a second phone if they have one, out of site and the car is the best place to hide that assuming you have a car each. Ask him randomly if you can borrow his car to go down the garage and see how reluctant he is to agree.

8) If he says he is with his mates, check their social media and see if they are out too. Alternatively, if he says he is with his friends' message one of their wives that night for whatever reason and drop in something about it.

9) If you ring him when he is away on business and he takes 2 minutes to reply he may be in restaurant and has gone outside to speak to you. Or he may be with her. If he explains too much about where he was and what he has done he may be guilty – over explaining is always a strong give-away.

10) Look at his car mileage before he leaves the house. When he returns reconcile that with what he says he has done that day.

11) He is likely to have a stock of Viagra with him if he is cheating, so see if you can see the side effects on him still when he returns home. A red chest is the easiest thing to look for.

12) If he is using another phone and it is in the house, search Bluetooth connections around you and see if an unknown device pops up.

A professional cheater

There are only two real ways to catch someone who is a clever cheater because even if you think you have "caught" them with multiple pieces of evidence they will always deny and deny it anyway. The first way, the most painful, is therefore to see it with your very own eyes. The second way is because the person who is cheating with, for want of a better word, goes "rogue".

A pro cheater will have thought it through, planned it, planned how to cover it up and a lot will certainly have Narcissistic Personality Disorder. I have known some in my time, they certainly exist but rarely talk about it unless they have split from their partner and have (once again apologies for trivialising this with one word) "retired" so can reflect backwards.

A professional man cheater will typically do these things

1) He will do it around his work hours or when you are away. He will avoid at all costs changing his routine or do anything that could arose your suspicion. He is conscious of any change in pattern or

behaviour.

2) He will never lie about his whereabouts in case you are tracking him remotely via a location app or indeed a tracking bug. So, if he says he has, say, a meeting in Norwich that's where he will cheat.

3) He will change pictures or make pictures up to prove where he was. With the rise of photoshop and other incredible image changing apps, a door has been left open for mankind to send you a picture with him superimposed into it, which really is incredibly tricky to spot it's a fake. It is that straightforward to change a picture and some even then have the audacity to post that fake image onto Instagram or Facebook.

You can change the time and date stamp of photos with various apps and even the location so if you happen to drag it into photos on your computer it will give you the false impression, he is telling the truth.

4) Most will simply have another phone they use and they will never use it in their car or at home and will leave it switched off until they need it. If he does just have the one phone, he will back that up to an encrypted hard drive (cost just £40 quid) and that is where he will read and look at "his trophies" as I mentioned above and he will save and delete everything before he gets home. He won't use iCloud at all or be connected to any family device. He will not have a password on his real normal phone as he wants you to check it and will openly leave it lying around almost "goading" you into it.

5) He won't have her number anywhere on his real phone.

6) He will probably check in with you if he is away before he starts the evening with his mistress to make sure you are actually at home and therefore won't just turn up. He will check that, for example, by asking to speak to one your children if you have any.

A professional cheater who is just really after sex will only ever see escorts. He will call from a new £5 sim card phone to the escort or have a fake email account and use a different name. He will always go to their place, never use his own hotel room.

The one thing he can't control though is the other "party".

The woman he is having an affair with may suddenly reveal all, which is always the biggest risk he faces. It is the only thing which is out of the hands of the professional cheater or indeed any cheater. The other woman who accepted his "rules" at the start becomes a loose cannon and is ready to blow the cement off his carefully built magnificent wall of lies, turning it all into tiny shameful, guilty, pieces of ugly rubble.

And herein lies mankind's or indeed anyone's adultery problem. When someone has an affair, the chances are the sex is not just great it is dangerously great and the best behaviour in general is always shown.

He will be unleashing an all-out romantic and erotic charm offensive onto his new prize catch so there is a strong possibility that his mistress will fall for him.

And then he is in trouble.

He will have set the plan out at the start. When to call, text, not to tell anyone, how to cover their tracks etc. and he will reinforce that each time he meets with her. But whatever "demands" he has set, to keep it a secret, it may all start to crumble the moment the butterflies start in her stomach and she falls for him.

Because he will have almost certainly have told her a load of man *bollo*cks which he almost certainly does not mean. He will have said things like he "*wishes he could be with her*" as he is "*so unhappy at home*", and that one day he "*will leave his wife for her*", that she is "*the best woman in bed he has ever had sex with*", that he "*thinks about her all the time*" and any other variation of words that will get him into bed with her.

And this is how stupid mankind is. Through his constant quest for the *PANDER* values, and a continued need to boost his insecure ego, he wants a woman to be all over him but by that very definition it would then mean they will have fallen for him.

And if you suspect him and have no evidence, what is he likely to do or say if confronted? Lie. He will turn the tables on you when confronted. He will get angry. He will go into unnecessary detail to explain why he wouldn't cheat. He won't logically try and allay your fears in anyway, he will generalise and stand his ground.

But say he has cheated and you get back together? There is no doubt, a reconciliation after any break up is euphoric. That first moment back together is like the honeymoon period at the start of your relationship. You gaze at each other, you can't believe you are together again, and the unbelievable, amazing, make up sex will make all those terrible events be forgotten in one incredible night of sexfest driven passion. But then that thing called reality will kick in and it's a hell of a long road back from reality let me tell you.

The absolute key to a reconciliation having any chance of working though is that something has to change to give it hope second time around. If nothing changes, you will get the same result and that second chance is totally and utterly doomed to fail.

Let's face facts if he has had an affair. You won't trust him ever again and he has the taste for cheating. That isn't a great foundation on which to build an already challenging relationship from. Even if how he cheated was a one-night stand done for "fun" it is still cheating. And what he did is almost certainly not a reflection on you at all it's a reflection on him. And on all mankind.

You are now after unconditional love but that will come with a bag full of justifiable new conditions which is almost impossible for him to fulfil in real life. And he is, remember, a man, and therefore by birth right an idiot.

Am I trying to say follow the advice in this book and he won't cheat on you? Nope. It may help deflect it though. May make him think twice that he "needs" too. And at the end of the day, for him and indeed for you, the grass is rarely greener on the other side. Doesn't matter if he mowed that grass in his mistress' bed 3 times a night, spraying lawn feed all over it, it still isn't greener. Except that is for a couple of nights right at the start of his affair when frankly, in those early moments, she is going to be better than you, because she is, well, a piece of grass that is greener in his *PANDER* led world

But soon that magical April, beautifully striped, Wimbledon Centre court grass that the affair started out to be played on will turn into a dark unattractive shade of ordinary brown in the endless hot summer sunshine. It then becomes just a regular bit of grass, just like marriage is on and off because you can't sustain "excitement" forever.

But you can refresh it and the annual review I mentioned previously may just give you that opportunity.

8 BREAKING UP

For better, for worse

For richer, for poorer

In sickness and in health

They are marriage vows, your emotions sealed into a legal contract of forever love. You skip along each day to the beat of cupid's intoxicating rhythm and then suddenly one of you decides they want a different song.

If you do, be careful what you wish for.

Imagine marriage or a long-term relationship as a huge boulder. You and your partner have managed to push it all the way to the top of a hill, over a period of time, worked hard at it, experienced many issues and challenges to get it there, but as a consequence of falling in wonderous love, by being an unbreakable team, you have reached the summit where it is then balanced nicely, just as your relationship will then be at that magical point.

One fateful day though, a storm arrives and you find yourself suddenly alone. But if you think clearly, just pause, you may still have enough strength to hold that boulder temporarily whilst you work out the best long-term plan to stop it from toppling over the edge of cupid's abyss. If you panic and rush around, raging at how unfortunate things are then before you know it, that storm has become a hurricane and the rock that was once your forever love is pushed over the top of that hill, hurtling down at a speed you cannot control and in a direction that sends it left and right until it smashes at the bottom, just like your marriage and your life will be if you allow it too.

During that descent downwards, you are no longer in control of anything. It all happens so fast, you make short term decisions that you wouldn't ever normally do, you can't think straight, logic totally disappears. Where once you were *dancing cheek to cheek*, you are now dancing rock to rock and they are thrown at frightening speed by everyone, your friends and vulture like lawyers who feed off the scraps of your once magnificent life.

Approximately 40% of all marriages now end in divorce and if you marry under the age of 20, only 3% apparently last until you die. So, at some point in your life, you will inevitably break up at least once from someone.

63% of divorces are initiated by a woman, which shows a lot about mankind. Women are two times mores more likely to start a divorce for unreasonable behaviour than men and 10% of marriages end because of adultery, though around 20% of people in marriages have committed adultery at some point. It is a lot to take in.

Before you even get to that point, you will undoubtedly have at some stage short term relationship break up issues to deal with, which by their very nature will be tackled differently in many ways to a long term one. The age you are at the time will also determine what happens next and what you should do as your man reacts to situations differently as he gets older. As I guess you do too.

If a man you have just met breaks up with you

Relationships that will last catch a wave at the beginning and that ride is breathtakingly wonderful. You don't want to get off and it rises and rises as momentum builds. You can't help yourself, nor can he. However, if the wave doesn't come then that's because it wasn't right to surf it in the first place, someone has said or done something that does not sit well or something isn't right in the overall dynamic between you.

Say you have had a few dates, maybe even slept together, but not quite boyfriend and girlfriend yet (as that is always traditionally defined). Then it just starts to fizzle out, you have this feeling he is losing interest, the time it takes for him to reply to your messages gets longer, the amazing things he said at the start get more ordinary and it just feels like he is going through the everyday motions.

A "single" man often likes to hedge his bets and if he hasn't said it is over to you, which he can easily do by message at that stage as he doesn't know you that well, then it's a good bet this is what he may be doing. Gut feeling will tell you. How do you react? Don't send him ultimatums, don't accuse him of playing you, don't show your feelings, don't sound desperate or needy. You can't make him jealous as a "weapon", he probably won't get that at this stage as emotions haven't started to build and of course there are no memories for him to miss so avoid "threatening" him with hints of other dates you may go on with other men, it won't work.

But if you really like him and he doesn't seem to feel the same way, what can you do? You obviously need to get another date, that date has to be magical but you need to be able to get one first.

Your choices are these

- Men react to something called Hero instinct. A damsel in distress. So, if you created a scenario that you needed his help for something and selected a few *PANDER* values as the reason then contact him on that basis.

- He will not react to jealousy but he will to envy. Post some great pics on social media looking wonderful and happy, not with other guys yet though, and this may bring out the desire in him once again.

- As shallow as this, I'm going to state the obvious here. If you have already slept together, lure him back with a naughty message. I know that romance and love aren't like that, but men are what they are.

At the end of the day, don't chase him after this or you will be asking for heartache. You deserve respect and attention and if he isn't giving it to you then it is his loss and move on.

If you have left him after a long-term relationship

It doesn't matter if you have left him for another man, or just walked away, a man goes through these stages in a break up.

Denial

Anger

Bargaining

Depression

Acceptance

And then possibly (with you at some stage)

Reconciliation

Effort

Men go onto hibernation following a break up, rather than opening up to their friends. Which is good because his mates don't want to hear it in detail either. They will simply not fuel the fire of hatred, there will not be endless chats on the phone, no plans to burn your clothes, no outpouring of emotions and tears will be saved for the very close one or two friends he has not to a wider group. He wants to keep some pride intact; all his *PANDER* values have been smashed to pieces.

There would not be endless nights of discussion with any other men, he would not read articles online about his feelings, about his mental state or how to try and get back with you. He is in the process of denial, a denial that he is not loved anymore.

He will back this up though with a total distortion of the facts to his friends.

"It was a mutual decision mate"

"I was planning on breaking up anyway, we just were not getting along"

He wants to show people that he is strong, that he is the bigger person.

Then anger will come. If you have cheated on him then "revenge" (if that is the right word) is unlikely to be against you. It won't be a social media onslaught, or a shitty message or email to the new bloke of yours, that just makes him look weak. It is highly likely, however, that vengeance may be considered against the man you cheated with and that could include being physical.

That is the first thing mankind's friends will say to him and every man knows someone who knows someone who knows someone who is a "hard man". That thought will go through his head even if he has no history of anything violent or physical and wouldn't dream of anything like that in normal life.

A recent study in America stated that 74% of men whose wife cheated on them thought seriously about a physical attack of some sort on the other man. That does not mean it will happen, far from it, but it is likely there would be confrontation and words shouted at some point.

After a break up, men often hit a period of depression and this is why they tend to quickly go into rebound relationships because they don't want to be left alone to deal with their feelings. At the same time, he needs instant *PANDER* to boost his self-esteem after rejection and therefore the rebound is unlikely to be the love of his life.

If your man has cheated on you, he is no longer doing it but you throw him out after discovering it

The advice I'm going to give you here is much easier said than done. Multiplied by a hundred. This advice is theoretical it is not street level. It reflects a perfect scenario where you are able to keep calm, whilst simply nothing else in your life is.

There is a poem by Kipling which describes the impossible task you face if he has left you for another women

If you can force your heart and nerve and sinew

To serve long after they have gone

And so, hold on when there is nothing in you

Except the will which says to them "hold on"

I know you hate him with every part of your destroyed body, but if you are crying at night then your emotions have not yet made their mind up. Half of marriages which break up result in a reconciliation at some point, even if you can't imagine that scenario at the outset.

Your brain is battling your heart. The pain has replaced the dream. But an hour after he has left, at that stage, deep down, you have only said goodbye with words. When your emotions catch up with those words then it is over but that can take a while because you will be in a state of trauma, have no doubt about that.

We see physical trauma. It's a leg break, it's a cut, it is visually right in front of us. No one sees an emotional one it is hidden inside the depths of our tortured soul. We know how to fix a body's injury and we know we will recover from it because a million operations have been done over a million years to prove just that.

Time is the only real way to fix an emotional trauma.

So, one minute after he has left, leave open that small window of opportunity for the possibility of a reconciliation.

But it is now you have to be careful what you say in that break up. You can't go back on it. Your chances of making a go of it in the future again with him will be affected if after you reconcile your friends truly hate him, your family hate him. Of course, they won't ever like him the way they did before and maybe never will at all but if you have exaggerated what he is like to prove your point then that will be hard to come back from.

At that moment, your friends will be screaming for vengeance it's a reflection of women wanting payback for thousands of years of mankind's arrogance, fair enough but that manifests itself in the constant back and forth between ladies when a "bad" break up happens.

He will be in denial. He will want you back. He will promise everything to you, say he will do anything to make up for it and how much he will change. He will take whatever you throw at him and agree with you. It is now a battle of tennis and as you play the anger serve he bats it back with a forehand of acceptance.

However, there is a timeframe by which mankind will then change tactic. He will eventually bat back your anger with anger and when that doesn't work he will play the rebound relationship backhand shot to make you jealous and so it will continue.

If he has left you for another women but you want him back

How do you need to react now to him?

SILENCE

Not revenge, not anger, not shouting

SILENCE

If you want to take anything from this book at all it is this. The whole point of understanding mankind is now. You haven't studied for this, it's a test no one has prepared you for. You only know how your heart is telling you to react but if you want to get back with your man, even after everything, then you must think as he does.

Mankind know that in a break up, women will close the circle with their friends and it is a terrifying sight and thought for a man. He knows what is coming to him, he is expecting the backlash, yet the *PANDER* he gets from his new women will be enough in the short term to withstand that.

Be noisy but truthful with your friends but be silent with him. Silence is defined as don't send message after message of anger and hate to try and make him feel guilty, it won't work. He has *PANDER* from his new women and that high now beats the low your messages will portray.

The absolute perfect thing to do is to totally and utterly ignore him. Anything other than that will just make him want to go to see his new women again because the choice is "ranting" you or the "excitement" that is her.

When he does sees you with someone else panic will set in and a period of self-reflection will happen. History will be viewed differently. I have had lots of chats where I have been told that men realise after a break up, they didn't communicate enough, weren't affectionate enough and the regrets will therefore come back eventually.

Because your emotions have turned into a tornado, the only thing that makes sense to you at that moment is to just vent the hurt you feel. For a woman, they will naturally turn to their friends and seek constant support, often many calls a day. They will read endless articles online about break ups but as far as I can tell, they were all not written by men and it is unlikely your close circle of friends will include a man either.

It is a cast iron fact that at some point

- He will miss his kids if you have any
- The short-term great sex with her is going to fizzle out

- The *PANDER* he gets from his new women will fade away

"*Absence makes the heart go fonder*" and it often does.

You have to give him a reason to remember the good times you once had and taking advice on men from other women just doesn't work. I do not say that in any arrogant way at all, I implore you to understand that and if you can objectively step back and think about it, having read everything I have written I hope you can see it.

I appreciate in your highly charged emotional state staying logical would not be easy, you want to vent all sorts of anger at whoever will listen. Yet the only way to have a chance of a reconciliation is to just take one deep breath and press pause on the remote control of your life.

Freeze your life and freeze your lips. Be silent. That pause will give you the greatest chance of recovering that logic and therefore the greatest chance of not only making another go of it, but a reconciliation that will last, regardless of the circumstances, regardless of the rights and wrongs.

We often feel that if we explain our point again and again, put it in writing, say it louder, we will be heard by our ex-partner but when the relationship breaks down, emotions are flared, and the ability to listen and engage diminishes greatly on all sides.

If you do reconcile though something has to change. There is a tendency to not want to discuss your issues as a new honeymoon period exists and you are walking on eggshells to try not to break it. But clearly something was wrong and if you want any chance of success then you must jump into that awkward discussion. The trouble with that once again though is mankind.

The growth of marriage councellors over the last few years is encouraging but men are not generally welcome participants in that. They do not like to discuss their feelings and issues with their close friends so they are even more reluctant to do that with a 3rd party.

But second time around with him, it is like all things, if you can solve the issues before it goes wrong it's a hell of a lot easier. If you give your car a service each year you maintain road worthiness, if you don't then one day you will break down in the middle of the M25 in rush hour. You can still get your car fixed, get home, but you are hit with massive stress, cost and disruption because you didn't tackle it before you started the journey that day.

And it is the same with all relationships.

God forbid if you have broken up, and are married then that awful thing called divorce is awaiting you. As if the hurt and pain of the split was not enough, along comes its more evil twin and whacks you on the head with a barrage of legal issues and court appearances.

My theory, and I'm not sure if I'm joking here, is that all married couples should sign a divorce agreement on the day they get married. That is romance for you right there.

"Do you, Nicola Tracey Jones, take Paul Andrew Smith to be your lawful married husband and do you agree to split everything 50-50 when divorce happens and split access to the kids fairly"

But think about it. At that moment, you are in love, you like each other, you are both reasonable, understanding, kind people who think rationally and show the right amount of respect to each other. You do not need anyone to make any decisions for you. When a divorce kicks in, everyone throws that rational thinking out of the window in the search for revenge, influenced by friends and solicitors.

Avoid it at all costs.

9 SEX

When you first meet your man, it is unlikely on that first date you will have a detailed discussion about sex.

How you like your steak cooked may come up in the romantic candlelight setting but how you like oral sex probably will not as you wait for the desert to arrive. But that lack of communication continues as the years pass, more often than not we just seem to let the whole sex thing evolve as the relationship grows avoiding any talk of "technique" or "fetish" that may be lurking in the secret vault section of our private minds.

And you won't find a sex section to complete in the online profile that you create on a normal dating site either. The typical template set out for you to fill in at the start may ask you to list your favourite movie or your ideal holiday but it won't ask you to define the size of a man's penis you are looking for.

Men don't chat to men either about detailed sexual things. There is never ever any discussion, for example, about how best to go down on a women or what position gets the most amazing orgasm. In the old days you may have got a chat about the "birds and the bees" from your dad and possibly some sex education in a general sense from school but no one ever teaches the fundamentals and there is no chance that any man would go to a friend and say

"I'm not sure how to suck a nipple properly mate, what do you suggest?"

So, mankind has taught themselves sex through trial and let's face it, mostly, error.

Men lead the way in this sexual communication void as they simply are not comfortable chatting to their partner about what they really might be thinking. At a basic level they are crudely open to their friends saying "*look at those tits mate*" but there isn't a chance in hell they would want to attend a male equivalent of an Ann Summers party. The image of someone passing around an anal vibrator within a gathered circle of men is certainly an interesting one but even the basic thought of buying underwear petrifies most of mankind.

Watching your partner enter Victoria Secrets should be a pay per view event. Get your friends around ladies, open up the Chardonnay and watch live for £4.99 as the helpless man nervously shuffles his way into his darkest nightmare. Living hell has arrived and Satan himself delivers the karma for all those times mankind has annoyed you.

He would be on his own, always on his own, he would never go into an underwear shop with another man. Ever. EVER. He is super cocky before he enters but when he steps over that lingerie line, he becomes a little lost tiny sheep for 15 minutes.

Mankind's strategy is to keep the head down and hope the size he wants is at the front of the rack because he knows if he has to sort through the range to find it, the ultimate disaster will then happen.

The ever so helpful shop assistant arriving next to him.

"Can I help you with anything sir, what particular things are you are looking for?"

No man in the world has ever replied to that with *"Yes, I want the g string set with a peek a boo baby doll and fishnet stockings please"*.

Which just happens to be the truth.

He can't even say *"no thanks I'm just looking"* as that just would sound like he is a pervert and almost certainly by now a lady will have come up beside him anyway to look at something too, which just heightens the feeling of being surrounded by a ménage à trois of utter embarrassment.

In today's world, if the American CIA want to torture someone, it is not waterboarding or being hung upside down for days in a secret hideout in Kazakhstan they should use, it's putting a man into a lingerie shop for half an hour.

Mankind know they cannot compete on the same level as a lady with lingerie. Men love lingerie, they are visual in their approach to many things, but it won't be the same in reverse unless I guess he started wearing the white naval officer uniform Richard Gere had on in *An and Officer and a Gentleman*.

If he came home from work like that, swept you up into his arms and took you away to a castle that night for dinner then fair enough you will be putty in his hands and you will swoon for days. But that's it. If he does it again the following week you would go along with it out of politeness I'm sure but by the 3rd time it would be

"FFS Jonny you aren't in the navy and you don't look like Richard Gere so act your age"

He can be romantic but he can't be seductive. He can't do his hair differently, he can't put make up on, he is what he is, the only contribution he could make to the evening's entertainment would be to actually have a shower beforehand.

So, with the lack of any tutor, increasingly mankind learns sex through porn and as men do not discuss detailed things about their home sex life with anyone, I have had to research this chapter a lot through doing just that myself. Men reading now will think that I'm the luckiest bloke on earth getting to study about porn for a job and on the flip side the sensible lot among you e.g., women, will be concluding that I'm just a dirty sad old pervert.

A tad harsh but I doubt you will believe me if I tried to plead my undoubted innocence.

What is even worse in my case though is that my search history at one point had all the sites looked at for this chapter. I had a new girlfriend at the time, we were getting on really well, until that is she asked to borrow my laptop to look at something. I frantically tried to grab the computer, looking very very shifty and got the natural question from her of

"Have you been emailing other girls behind my back?"

Which I could only defend myself with the worse defence in mankind history

"Other girls?! I replied full of utter indignation *"I would never do that with you I am loyal I don't want anyone else in my life but you. I've just been looking at porn for 48 hours that's all"*

Why do men watch porn? Sexual excitement is the obvious reason. Men and intimacy are not often a perfect fit. Intimacy involves listening, building and developing a relationship with oneself that's open, understanding, honest, cherishing and most importantly, loving. After this you then develop a willingness to being completely open with others, which is what being intimate really is about; being fully transparent without boundaries, barriers or controls.

The problem with intimacy is that it is a choice (although this is also an intrinsic part of its beauty). We either choose to build and bring it to ourselves, getting to know the source of love which we have inside of ourselves and share it, or we don't and we end up seeking a replacement for this from outside sources.

In other words, Porn

78% of men watch it in the US apparently (73% in the UK) and 38% of women (36% in the UK). A man's view on sex is therefore best understood in today's world by looking at what he searches for on porn sites.

An online survey said that 28% of men under 50 masturbate at least once a week. And Porn will more often than not play a leading role in replacing you during that private mankind moment.

Pornhub is one of the leading content providers in the world and they have 100 million people land on their site every day. In other words, that's over 36 billion visits per year. It is bigger than any TV show, any sports broadcast, any soap opera, anything you can ever watch on TV.

Helpfully, in relation to this chapter, Pornhub publish an annual summary of current trends and it is here that your mind needs to open up to the reality of what mankind is actually doing behind the scenes. Hence the need for my research. Honest.

I have analysed their 2022 findings. Stripping out those categories obviously searched for by teenagers (MILF etc) and excluding local country specific areas (e.g., Japan), the adjusted top 3 for men and women were

Most searched categories (out of about 60) by men were
1) Lesbian
2) Anal
3) Threesome

And astonishingly the top 3 women searches (again out of about 60 categories) were
1) Lesbian
2) Threesome
3) Anal

The "trending" searches by men on Pornhub specifically is fascinating.

1) Reality e.g. a clip not involving a porn star as such but an amateur grew by 169%
2) Group Sex was up 34%
3) Outdoor sex was up 121%
4) Feet were up 38% (see below)
5) Pegging (see below) up 28%
6) Cuckhold (see below) up 18%
7) Bondage up 18% and into Pornhub's top 20 list for the first time (see below)

Bet you were dying to know all that.

So here goes, all this "wisdom" needs translating into some sort of mankind rational for your education and amusement so I have selected a few areas to showcase man's sexual thoughts

Anal

To anal or not to anal that is the question.

It is what Shakespeare wanted to say I'm sure but he chose all those romantic words instead.

I don't know how else to begin this part other than to say that mankind would love it if you did apparently. But they totally get why you would not and absolutely this should not be considered if a lady does not want to. This is borne out by my private survey where 64% said they would like to have anal sex with their partner, or at least try, but 91% said it wasn't that important in the overall dynamic of life.

Thank God for that.

It is likely therefore that if a man is ever offered the chance of anal sex by his wife or girlfriend, then the first reaction will always be total disbelief with the word, *"Really ??"* arriving very soon after. He will be genuinely very shocked. He will start to believe in Father Xmas all over again. It is according to studies the holy grail for a mankind in a "normal" sexual relationship with his partner.

The sexual stats point to that as well. It is growingly more common in a relationship. In a large-scale survey in the UK, 42% of men said they had tried anal sex with their partner. 38|% said they had in my private survey. Very similar.

Why do men like it so much, or at least the fantasy of it?

It is because anal sex avoids intimacy and focus' solely on the act itself. It is not an emotional thing; it is being naughty, raw and very daring. Mankind feel dominant when they do it. It is nothing to do with the tightness of a women's vagina whatsoever, that is never an issue for man as I explained before.

There is also reverse anal to consider, which is called "pegging". I can't put this any other way than by describing it in brutal honesty: it is when a lady wears a strap on and fucks her man in the arse. What I can firstly say is that it is virtually never discussed by heterosexual mankind. I have heard it only once and when the guy in question in the man cave one night said *"he couldn't be with a woman unless they did that to him every time"*, the whole room stopped what they were doing. Every one of the 10 or so men in there that evening looked uncomfortable and stared at their feet.

He explained how in love he was with a girl he had dated the previous night and the basis for that was solely on the fact that after a few drinks they decided to go back to her place. After a bit of sensual touching, ear nibbling and gentle stroking she then, without warning, had rammed her middle finger into his arse and carried on as if nothing had happened. Now she struck gold with him but I'm not sure that would have got the same reaction from most men.

First date advice for ladies. Don't talk about your mother. Don't talk about babies. Avoid fingering a man's arse.

Anal sex is a real pressure situation for mankind though because it requires a very good erection. If his knob is soft then he doesn't have much option other than to try and fold it in half and push it in the best he can. You were expecting pain and it didn't hurt at all.

That's because only a few inches of rolled up knob has just been manoeuvred into you.

Threesome/Lesbian

The Kinsey Institute in America from a survey of 5,000 people aged 18 to 70 reported that 95% of men and 87% of women had fantasised about a threesome and that 28% of men had actually had one. It is in the top 3 categories for both men and women on the Pornhub survey.

Doing it is now apparently is just as common as owing a cat.

There are 2 types of threesomes if you are in a relationship with the opposite sex. One with 2 women and a man (FFM) and one with two men a woman (MMF). This is where sexual hypocrisy once again arrives. In a heterosexual man's world, the vast majority would only consider a threesome with two women and him, so bi sexuality for mankind should only apply to his partner.

However, bringing in someone else to your sexual dynamic is hugely risky even if it is another woman not a man. The thought of FFM is a visual pleasure for mankind. It isn't necessary about the thought of him having sex with another women, it is seeing his wife with one.

The reversed *PANDER*

A man needs *PANDER,* to be "powerful", confident and yet where sex is concerned there is a rising trend which gives mankind the complete opposite feeling. It all involves man's humiliation effectively and the sexual arousal he gets from that.

It's the right side of the brain fighting the left side and that fight stimulates arousal.

Apparently.

This can include bondage. 27% of couples say that at least one of the partners in a relationship likes to be tied up and dominated in that way, as in 50 Shades of Grey. Bondage usually involves a safe word, something that can be said if matters get out hand. A very sensible, responsible approach I have to say though can I be the sexual voice of reason here and point out the bleeding obvious.

If it hurts, just say stop.

But a safe word, a hidden code, is cooler, more daring. However, remember mankind is not as clever as he makes out.

To highlight this, I read a story online in the process of writing this book that I must share with you. A guy had arranged a bondage session with his wife and another man at a hotel. As part of that "thrill" the plan was for him to wait in the bar downstairs and listen in to the shenanigans going on in the room via his phone.

The problem, *quelle surprise*, was the man wasn't listening properly to his wife when she told him what the safe word was. When the action started it suddenly dawned on him as he was alone in the bar downstairs listening in, that he had no idea of what it was at all.

So up in the lift he went to the rescue, not the kind of knight in shining armour Disney had envisaged but a modern-day hero nonetheless, entered, tapped on the shoulder of the man administering a whip to his tied up, gagged, wife and said

"Ever so sorry to interrupt but what was the safe word again?"

Ten minutes later lounging on the sofa by the bar with the safe word *"apple"* duly remembered he heard his wife on the audio from the room upstairs say

"aafuauuauagggle"

He sat up. *"My God, was she saying apple? It could have been apple."* He turned the volume up and out came that word again

"aafuauuauagggle"

So up in the lift he went again to the rescue, once again not the kind of knight in shining armour Disney had envisaged but a modern-day hero still nonetheless, once again entered, tapped on the shoulder of the man administering a whip to his tied up, gagged wife and said

"Ever so sorry to interrupt but did my wife just say the safe word?"

His wife was not happy. *"aafuauuauagggle"* wasn't "apple" apparently it was the noise she was making as she was close to orgasm and he had just interrupted the good part.

Along the same lines, 13% of men fantasise about BDSM (Bondage, Domination, Submission, Masochism). Essentially this involves not only humiliation but pain as well, ranging from candle wax being poured over you to having your nuts kicked in by a Nazi boot wearing dominatrix.

This is one of the reasons a man will therefore see an escort. On adultwork there are 3,184 ladies who will provide BDSM so the demand is most certainly there.

Now that's a conundrum discovering your man likes that during your relationship. If 8 years into your marriage you are told over lasagne one night that he likes electrodes put on his nudgers and 10 volts pumped through them, you may feel somewhat aggrieved this wasn't disclosed before you said *"I do"*.

And who said romance was dead.

Cuckhold

Cuckholding is the act in which a man or woman enjoys watching their partner having sex with someone else. The word 'cuckold' is based on the cuckoo bird, which disguises its eggs in other birds' nests and leaves them to take care of the hatchlings.

It is somewhat different from a MMF threesome in that it is especially designed to "humiliate" the man. He wants his girlfriend/wife to tell him how wonderful this new man is at it triggers "safe sexual jealousy" in him and gives him reverse *PANDER* excitement.

Surveys say 58 percent of men and one in 3 women have fantasied about it. There are over 53,000 videos of it on Pornhub and many have had over a million views per clip.

But this is the ultimate risk-taking relationship thing you can do. Not only are you confronting jealousy but also humiliation and the post sex reaction may not be the same as that achieved in the actual moment itself.

Be very careful what you wish for.

Feet

Now this area of sexual fetish, seemingly on the rise in mankind's list of turn ons, was a huge surprise to me as not once in any year, in any day, in any situation, have I heard any man say the words

"cor look at the feet on her"

So off I went into Pornhub again, on your behalf of course and definitely not because I wanted to look at porn once more perish the thought, and I have discovered that of the 161,234 clips you can watch if you type in "Feet" on that site, the sexual fantasy relates to two things

- the smell of the feet
- getting masturbated by a lady's feet and not her hands

Sexual arousal can be triggered by numerous things, not just "fancying" someone. It is more likely to be visual but also includes the touch of certain clothes e.g. silk or satin or the smell of something e.g. underwear. So, I can rationally understand that the smell of feet do turn some people on and watching a porn clip of a man smelling a ladies feet, with no actual intercourse going on, is part of the new age sex on the rise and each to his own as I've said before.

As long it isn't illegal and both parties are Ok with something then why the hell not.

But what I found astonishing was the fact some ladies can actually masturbate a man with their feet and there are thousands of clips on that in Pornhub, some with over ½ a million views. I watched a few and I have to say not because I was personally turned on, but because I was in total amazement and awe at the coordination it takes to do anything with your feet it is some skill. It also requires a certain degree of fitness as the lady lays back and does leg rises with a penis between her feet for several minutes.

It is maybe something for a lady to consider with her partner therefore I helpfully suggest.

You can get fit at the same time as pleasing your man and you could even read a book in the same moment as you are laying down anyway and your hands are free.

New age sex

The definition of "Sex" is now changing rapidly because of the wide list of categories offered by porn sites. A "fetish" or "kink" in the old days was some bondage rope and a whip, now it can include watching people blow their noses or being dressed up in clown costumes jumping on balloons. Non-penetration sex is arriving fast and the demand is apparently out of control.

Pornhub note that sexuality is coming out of the shadows. Our curiosity is widening and being influenced by things we didn't even know we liked or would consider in the first place. As three quarters of men watch porn the demand for this fetish type sex will increase because the number of films being made in those areas will rise and rise. And those films are not now being produced by large porn studios in LA or London, they are being made on phone cameras by everyday people men and women alike.

And men can now get customised videos made through sites like "*only fans* "and "*admire me*" It is mass produced digital sex and it's like the wild west out there. What can happen now is that ladies in the sexual services industry make a custom film for £25 on anything the man wants. It is widely offered and whilst it is not on amazon prime just yet, within 24 hours you can have a digital download of a lady going to the loo to watch at your leiaure.

Which reminds me of a story a friend once told me. He had arranged to see an escort in a hotel and she mentioned to him at the start "would he like to see her urinate?". He was so I am told quite excited at the prospect of his first *golden shower* which is essentially when a lady urinates over him for sexual pleasure. You may laugh or indeed be shocked but there are 80,361 film clips on Pornhub on that very subject so it is my "duty "once more as mankind's self-appointed spokesperson to inform you about this very fascinating subject.

Off he went to the bathroom got a load of towels and laid them over the bed. In glorious Hugh Heffner posing mode he draped himself over the sheets and waited for the flowing fountain to be sprayed all over him. He waited. And waited. She totally ignored him. Instead off she went around the hotel room pissing on things. Yep, you heard that right. She pissed on the sofa, the carpet even the curtains. Then she got the kettle and pissed into that as a grand finale.

Stunned silence from my mate.

She apparently had a fetish for hotel room pissing to leave her "mark" just like a cat in your garden does. But whereas a cat will leave a scent in the geraniums this escort left one on the curtains in the hotel room. Imagine inviting her round for dinner, in between courses she pisses in your fish tank and sits back down waiting for the desert to arrive.

And there are 8,191 video clips of women urinating in hotel rooms or changing rooms on Pornhub. Dare you to quote that when you meet your friends for coffee tomorrow, that will certainly bring out a different chat to the normal one you have in Starbucks.

Of course, some of these fetishes you will just laugh at and so did I. But each to his own. There was however one custom clip I found which had a lady with her shoes full of baked beans and was running on a treadmill, which had over 25,000 views. I laughed at first of course I did. But then I thought hang on if this is mankind asking a woman to humiliate herself and be paid for it then that line is most certainly not acceptable. If a consenting woman in a relationship doesn't mind doing that for "her man", and of course if a man doesn't mind doing whatever a lady gets turned on by then what's the harm it's sexual arousal not abuse.

But the line is drawn where a man almost forces a woman to do something she is not comfortable with and that is just simply wrong and is what has gone on for the last 25,000 years no doubt.

So, we are in a sexual revolution and it is clear from my survey we still don't talk properly about it. Every online study on relationships will say communication is one of the top things everyone wants. Yet when it comes to pretty much one of the top 3 things in a relationship, sex, we don't bother to get to the bottom of what really might turn us on. The danger of that is you may well have been willing to try a fetish or kink but if your man won't tell you about it, he may turn to an escort to get it and there are thousands to choose from in the UK right now.

The discussion on sex should be done regularly because sexual desires do change. The problem is of course that there is a huge sensitivity to either partner looking like a complete pervert or we don't want to appear to be criticising the other side by suggesting trying another way to do "xyz".

If you are brave enough, include sex in the annual review I suggested. I have put into Appendix one what that could look like.

What is certain though is sex has a whole new meaning. Prepare for sexual evolution because it has arrived into our life's

10 NARCISSISM

Prepare to be tortured.

The word Narcissism at first glance conjures up an image of a pruning man in front of a mirror inspired by Carly Simons *Your So Vain* song principally about Warren Beaty, a totally understandable and reasonable dig directed at all of mankind. But, now, in this modern-day world it has a more sinister meaning, which extends far beyond just looking at yourself in the mirror a lot.

Narcissistic Personality Disorder (NPD)

NPD is sometimes accompanied by its slightly nicer sidekick Borderline Personality Disorder (BPD) but both usually trigger something called *gaslighting* which is fast becoming not just a Hollywood script but a part of everyday normality.

NPD effects at least 5-7% of the population and 68% of those are men. There are 32m men in the UK and so that means at the top end there are 1.5m men in Britain who have this disorder, which is a staggering number as very few people know about it or what it means. Google NPD and 24 million hits come up.

BPD effects around 4% of the population and 75% of those people are women.

Before we begin to get into this chapter I need to emphasis one thing. There is a difference between your man being a complete arse on and off and him being a narcissist. Most of it is down to common sense but sometimes it is hard to spot, and the problem with this disorder is that if you spot it too late in your relationship, then all hell will break lose at some point and there isn't must you can do to defend yourself emotionally at the onslaught that comes with it.

What I am about to write is real life and it's happening all around us. I am an expert on NPD and BPD and have chatted to hundreds of victims and there is an astonishing similarity in cases because people with these disorders follow very similar patterns.

You might not have recognized that your husband was a narcissist when you first met him and started dating. In fact, there is a good chance that he came along and swept you off your feet. Narcissists tend to be very romantic at the start. Which makes it even more difficult to identify Narcissistic Personality Disorder as they know how to make you feel good, it's incredibly manipulative but you will be so caught up in the newness and fun of the relationship that you won't notice it.

I will explain the significance if your partner has one of these disorders but does your partner show any of these things, constantly, not just in a one-off situation.

- Lack of empathy
- Lack of real interest in your life and achievements
- In need of and requiring constant admiration
- Exaggeration of achievements and talents
- Possessing a sense of entitlement
- Sets totally unrealistic goals that cannot really be achieved
- Has an arrogance about him, he will belittle you and blame it on his sense of humour with a typical *"that's just me being silly"* reply when you get offended by something
- Totally unemotional when problems ever arise

I must repeat this is constantly, or regularly. Every one occasionally gives off any of these characteristics, is it part of your everyday life. But if its constant then they are showing the signs of having NPD.

The problem is individuals with NPD are unable to realize the damaging effect their behaviour is causing and it is not an easy discussion to bring up. Behind this mask of extreme confidence in someone who has NPD lies a fragile self-esteem that is vulnerable to the slightest criticism.

If your man has experienced any sort of trauma as a child, ranging from generally feeling unloved by one or more of his parents or been subject to any physical or sexual abuse then the NPD problem is highly likely to be coming because these disorders manifest at that stage.

NPD should not be confused with high self-confidence and self-esteem which occur often in mankind of course. Narcissism is not narcissism as you know it, it is much deeper than that.

All relationships with a Narcissist follow this pattern

Idealisation

The first stage in a narcissistic relationship is perhaps the most dangerous of them all as this is when they in effect hook you into their world.

The idealisation phase though always occurs right at the beginning of any relationship. They will make you feel truly special, they will shower you with love and adoration and present themselves to be exactly who they think you want them to be. They are typically very clever, with a sixth sense of knowing what it is you want.

During this phase, you may find that you just can't get enough of this person. Being around them is intoxicating, and you may not believe that you have finally found someone that is so "in tune" with you. You may be wined and dined at amazing restaurants, taken on great dates, showered with thoughtful gifts, and receive constant "love notes" telling you how perfect and special you are.

At his point it could well be, and hopefully is, just two people falling in love with each other.

But because they have made you feel so good, you may just ignore some of the warning signs that start to become obvious, ever so slowly. But because you like him so much now, even if a few "red flags" start to appear, you quickly explain away the narcissist's poor behaviour away.

Devaluation

After you are completely drawn in, the narcissist in your life is going to begin changing the rules of a normal relationship and the manipulation will start. It will be subtle at first but over time, and this could even be over a number of years, the narcissist will ramp up their antics to deceive, twist and distort facts. They will lie to you and they are expert liars.

They may become sarcastic about you in front of others to "put you in your place", lower your self-esteem and make themselves appear more "powerful". They may become aggressive and often rage at you to shock you into submission. At the worst, they may even become physically abusive. They will almost certainly cheat on you.

Despite this, it is common to continue making excuses for them. This is partially because you have become so enamoured with them in the first phase, but also because they will keep throwing a little love-bombing into the mix of abusive tactics to keep you spellbound by them. And it usually works I'm afraid to say, because they also throw in a thing called bread crumbing where the crumbs of affection you get make up for their behaviour as you crave their love so much still.

The manipulative tactics that the narcissist uses will cause you to start doubting yourself and your sanity; and you may even find yourself living in a fog of confusion. You may feel like you just aren't good enough and can't do anything right. Your self-esteem will be stripped away and you will be forever walking on eggshells trying to appease the person who once made you feel incredibly special.

Discard

The narcissist is always looking for what's in it for them and after the devaluation the discard phase isn't just a break up, it's break up designed in the furnaces of hell itself.

Once the narcissist believes you are no longer providing the "supply" they need, or if you have undermined their sense of false self-worth in any way, that rug you swept all those red flags under will be ripped right out from under you and in a devasting way. You will be discarded and replaced with a new "model" they can use to feed their ego.

They will discredit you. They will turn all your happy times into things that never happened. They will project all the things they are and have done wrong onto you. If they had an affair, suddenly it turns out you did not them. They will flatty just abandon you, block you, ignore you and their cruelty in the break up is beyond human.

One of two things will happen after you have been discarded. They may leave you alone if their new "supply" is worthy of them, or they may at some point try and hoover you back into their lives. They will use any means necessary to get you back in order to recover the control over you they once had.

Because they are expert liars, they will have no short-term shame in begging, crying, guilt-tripping, blame-shifting and making false promises of how much they have changed to win you over.

There is a thing called Stockholm syndrome where a victim of horrific abuse can still have positive feelings towards their "captor". They are in denial that this is the person who put them in that situation and in their mind, they think this is the person who is going to still give them true love. And this is why so often a victim of narcissism allows that narcissist back into their lives despite everything that has happened.

But the cycle of abuse won't stop and once they've lured you back in with their charm, the narcissist will fall right back into the devaluation phase and so it begins all over again. A narcissist will not change their ways, they need narcissistic "supply" to exist and will find that supply in any way they can.

Effects of Living with A Narcissist Husband

You Lose Your Outside Relationships

A narcissistic husband does not want you to have any relationships. He will work to pull you away from your friends and family slowly.

It could start by him making small comments about how he doesn't like your friends. He might always *need* to spend time with you when you're supposed to go out with them so you'll choose to stay with him instead.

His sense of entitlement over your time will grow. You start spending more time with him and relying on him to meet your needs. The more this happens, the less time you spend with others, and eventually it feels like you have lost your relationships with everyone.

While feeling completely embraced by your partner, it might be hard to understand the gravity of an emotionally abusive relationship. And without your outside relationships to help, that will just get harder.

A narcissistic husband will whittle away at your self-esteem. Narcissists can't handle when someone else does something better than them. They can't handle admitting that they're wrong. That means that you are never going to be the one that is right within the relationship. You will be criticized and belittled. Eventually, this constant criticism will impact your confidence and you will become a shell of the person you once were.

You will start to feel that you are "not good enough" or "worthy" of your man. Because he is secretly insecure himself, his goal is to build himself up and make himself feel better by making it seem like he's more capable than you.

People with NPD will also thrive on the idea that they are out of your league, that you should not leave them, because they are the best you'll ever get. Their sense of entitlement over the relationship will make you feel like you would be stupid to leave.

When your man is a narcissist, your life will become all about making him happy. You will learn how to say and do things to boost his ego because you can't stand the way he behaves when you don't. It could be that he becomes depressed, angry, irritable, or verbally abusive. After seeing this behaviour, time and time again, you learn how to give him what he wants.

This isn't *PANDER*, this is abuse.

Over time, you start to lose yourself. The dreams and goals that you had for your own life will slowly start to disappear because your man controls so much of your life. A narcissist cannot handle admitting that they are wrong which means even if you know they were wrong, and they know they are wrong, they will still not apologize.

Their sense of self-importance will overpower any scenario. Every argument that the two of you have will end with you taking the blame for it. Everything is your fault, even things that are outside of your control. They may say that you're doing everything wrong - even small things like grocery shopping or laundry - and tell you that if only *you'd* change, the marriage would be "perfect."

Gaslighting

Gaslighting, a movie that came out in 1944 portrayed a husband manipulating his wife to make her think she was losing her sense of reality so he could commit her to a mental institution and steal the inheritance which had been left to her.

The worrying thing about gaslighting is that it is highly likely to not be planned like a Bond Villain would, it is "simply" a result of a mental disorder your partner has, more typically NPD or BPD.

It is designed not only to "torture" but also to divert you from what is really happening making you doubt your own mind to such an extent you wonder what is real and what is not. It starts slowly, with say a picture being moved out of place, the questioning of your memory of an event, trivialising your concerns on anything strange.

The first few times someone tries to change your reality, you will likely not believe them and may tell them that they're wrong or they have misunderstood the situation. The more someone gaslights you, the more you begin to question whether the gaslighter has a point, but you will still try to defend yourself. You will try to disprove their statements with logic or try to reason with them, but you will try to "be fair" and see it from their point of view as well.

After a while though, you may believe them. The more the gas lighter can keep you feeling insecure and questioning your reality, the more you'll believe their explanations. Over time, you reach a point where your self-confidence is destroyed, and you no longer trust yourself.

"You are wrong, that never happened", "stop being paranoid", "stop overreacting" will be their standard words in any argument.

You want to believe your partner so you give them the benefit of the doubt that they could never do that to you, which will lead you to believing it must be your mind and your issue to resolve therefore.

Extreme examples of gaslighting are downright worrying and because it is so extreme you will find it often hard to get people to believe you as it is very tricky to prove. If your man is gaslighting you then that is domestic abuse at the very highest level.

Borderline Personality Disorder

As a conclusion to this dark chapter, there is an offshoot to NPD and it's called Borderline Personality Disorder, which occur in women more than men. So even though this book is focused on mankind, it is worth a few pages outlining this disorder because it will have a huge effect on your relationship if it develops in later life.

But this disorder, far easier than with NPD, can be managed and treated if you recognise it within you.

BPD usually arises from some sort of trauma sufferers experienced in their childhood and it often lays dormant for many years. It is an intense fear of abandonment which makes you take extreme measures to protect yourself if you feel someone you deeply love is about to leave. BPD will then trigger a *"false self"* to appear and it becomes a Jekyll and Hyde gladiatorial duel within the very depths of your brain. This second and dark personality tries to take over you and as they increasingly surface and increasingly win that fight, they embark on a reign of cruelty against their partner without any guilt, shame or fear of the consequences, akin to someone with NPD.

Many celebrities are reported to have BPD but none have come out openly and said it. Amy Winehouse, Princess Diana certainly showed many traits if the stories about them are to be believed and it has been widely reported that Elizabeth Taylor did too, which would explain the constant desire for jewels and attention.

It is the result of complex trauma which in effect splits the brain into two. The left side, the "logical" part has a battle with the right side which is "emotion" and eventually the right side wins forcing the sufferer of BPD to become a highly rebellious illogical "child" trying to deal with unresolved trauma memories from years before. In order for them to heal, the left and right side have to finally "grow up" which will then create a stable balanced relationship where both are aligned and in tune with each other. Anyone who has suffered an abusive childhood be that mental or physical and who becomes very unstable as a result some years later should not be seen as a surprise case.

What happens in childhood for anyone suffering neglect or abuse is that the terrible disorder lays dormant. For BPD sufferers it is more likely generated from a lack of love from their father or mother where they were screaming out for it. They were in effect emotionally abandoned but as a child they couldn't fight back, couldn't realise the inner rage they wanted art that time so it lays silent and returns when they feel abandonment coming again.

Think back to your early childhood.
You can probably conjure up some really positive memories. Running with friends, learning in school, playing new games, etc. As a child, life is generally pretty simple and you have the love of your parents around you and you need that feeling of love and of their protection and the fact they are there for you when you need them and they won't let you down.

But say for example your mum, when you grew up, never really took an interest you, would belittle you, would ignore you if they were with your friends, wouldn't really help you with your homework or want to sit with you at night, preferring the company of say your brother who was a similar age. You want as an 8-year-old to shout out that you feel abandoned and need love but you can't because you are 8 and you haven't got the courage or belief anyone will listen.

This feeling sits with you, inside you, dormant and when you next meet a grade "A" person `e.g. your husband` and have a love for him akin to the love you had for your parents, you are at risk of this disorder arriving the moment you feel that you might be abandoned again.

Those with BPD never developed these emotional coping skills. As a result, every emotion they feel is intense. Their highs are absolutes, their lows are absolutes. They resort to extreme lengths to get what they want, and generally lack empathy for those they care about. Unable to take responsibility for their actions, they blame everyone else for their faults. Unable to control their emotions, they lash out towards you in extreme anger. They may call you names, say things that aren't true, or self-harm. Many lack self-awareness and are physically unable to see how they have harmed those around them. Others realize their errors, and hate themselves even more for it. They may see you as the perfect significant other in one moment, and treat you as less than dirt a few hours later. At the end of the night, they won't even remember what happened, or get why you're upset at them for blowing up. They have difficulty processing middle grounds.

But that doesn't help the victim when the onslaught comes. Confronting anyone with BPD the way you would normally deal with problems is a total disaster waiting to happen because BPD sufferers can't take that "confrontation" in any rational way. But unless you know that, you carry on as any other "normal" person would do and therefore you keep heading towards a massive truck in your tiny car, in a game of chicken that you will never win.

It truly is a sad disorder and summed up by this sufferer who wrote to me

We want someone who will love us unconditionally.

When we push them away, we want them to come back.

We will push them to their limits and drag them through our roller coaster of emotions. And when they finally can't take it anymore we will say that we knew they would leave just like everyone else.

But we don't want them to leave. We want that one person who is willing to stay and love us forever no matter what hell we put them through.

11 LBJ

You all know the saying the way to man's heart is through is stomach

Which we all now know is complete nonsense, instead you travel past his stomach about 20 inches and get to the place you will really win everything.

Of course, lovely food, cooking together is wonderful and helps to build the foundations that is needed in any relationship. Friendship, laughter, camaraderie, romance they all play a massive part in building that house of love. However, as shallow as this is to say, sex gives you an advantage: foundations will give you long term stability.

In a recent study, 48 percent of men indicated that feeling desired was "essential." in a relationship. And desired means sex, or the hint of sex. And that means this word.

Oral sex.

More commonly known to the 5 billion philistine men on this planet as The Blow Job.

Not a very sexy phrase though is it or indeed technically correct as there isn't much blowing going on, it's the reverse, it's sucking. But the term "blow" arrived in the 1950's apparently to crudely describe "blowing your load".

Le Blow Job (*LBJ*) would sound better though don't you think. Anything with a "*Le*" or "*La*" before it is so subtly sexual that it just purrs from your lips like a cat in an orgy of cuddles from their owner. God damn those *Frenchie's* they are *sooooo* cool.

Or to put it another way

Voulez vous coucher avec moi

Now, these next few pages as we discuss *LBJ* may be a tad controversial in our new found friendship so please take a deep breath, get yourself a Gin and Tonic and just remember I'm honestly trying to help, it's not my fault mankind is as they are.

Let's start with me saying the following which will have me hung from every Guardian reader's rooftop as a male idiot and you will never find in any women magazine written by a lady because it is not what society wants to believe.

LBJ is more often than not the single most important thing in a man's life. Ok not after his kids or his love for you but in his daily life, his weekly life, its' something that is on his mind. A lot.

It therefore will affect your relationship with him massively. It doesn't mean the end of it if you don't, doesn't mean he won't love you if you don't, but if you understand that on and off throughout his life it simply is, then you will go a long way to not only keeping your man "happy" but also "making" him be the attentive, romantic person you want him to be.

To put it another way, you have to give a dog a bone and he will follow you.

This is why we may have just fallen out within each other. But take a deep breath. I am not saying all this as a male chauvinistic pig expecting his women to perform sex acts because it is their "duty", of course it isn't that is totally unacceptable. But mankind has developed this way over millions of years and whilst society has changed, values have changed, the way women are quite rightly now seen as (more than) equal to a man, the simple and basic fact is that a man is so often driven by his cock, because of *PANDER*.

So, to a very large extent it therefore means he is driven by *LBJ*.

Please do not shoot the messenger I'm on your side and it is pretty appalling when you think about it I know. But I've promised to give you warts and all in this book and so continuing down this shallow righteous path I must go.

Let me present some sound evidence for the bleeding obvious I have just written. The bleeding obvious that society understandably doesn't want to write about as it taints the romantic Disney dream of relationships.

But look back over the years. Julius Caesar gambled his Roman empire on his desire for Cleopatra. Henry VIII had six wives. King Edward VIII abdicated in 1936 because of Wallis Simpson. Look at Bill Clinton and Monica Lewinsky. Look at JFK and Marilyn Monroe. Even the Beatles broke up because of John Lennon's fascination with Yoko Ono. I'm sure of course there was love and romance in there somewhere, but essentially all those men were led by their desire for sex.

No one cheats on a woman because he wants to taste a better pie than his wife makes. He makes that totally terrible, illogical decision because of his knob, who is in fact mankind's spokesperson for *PANDER*. When Bill Clinton had an affair with Monica Lewinsky it wasn't because she made a good steak it was because he wanted *LBJ*.

That is the President of the USA we are talking about, the most powerful man in the world.

Scary.

If it's any consolation, I think mankind's logic does improve as he gets older but it is still at the forefront of his mind even in later life. So, that is still billions and billions of decisions being taken every day by a man's sexual thoughts.

Uber Scary.

Ok, having now been convinced hopefully of my well-argued and intellectually thought through rational that the even the debating society of Oxford University would be proud of, let me try and set out and explain the impact of that conclusion.

Men are even more idiotic, selfish and juvenile than you thought they were before you started to read this book.

However, let's have some fun with all this, why not. I'm making a point as best I can because you need to reflect on it, but let's consider everything in a light hearted way so we depart as friends when you finish the final page.

LBJ is the ultimate tool of seduction and tease, it will make your man worship you more than anything else you could ever do in your entire relationship. It can also kick start your relationship in any situation. It is the ultimate "tool of power" a woman has and unlike anything mankind can "offer" a lady as a single act. If a man says to you that he will give you oral

sex tonight you will think ok that's probably nice and a thoughtful gesture, almost sexy, but it will never come close to having the same effect in reverse if you say that to a man.

As simplifying life and love as that statement is, as much as it would have Shakespeare cringe at the very thought of the Romeo and Juliet love story being tainted with Johnsons shallow conclusions, giving one and being good at it therefore will help along the way with your man.

Le blow job (LBJ) is not an Olympic sport. No one can judge who is the best but frankly as we are on the subject I started, is it more impressive to suck a knob well or throw a Javelin 80 meters into a bit of grass to win a Gold Medal??

The way to a man's heart is through his stomach, is a phrase still very much used even in today's new age. The naïve old romantics amongst us would like to think this was true and of course, having nice food is a wonderful thing. No man is ever going to object to a lovely home cooked supper and it adds to the friendship, the comrade, the soft feeling of love inside you which grows over the longer term. It is one of the fundamentals of building a lasting relationship, one of the everyday simple things that we take for granted but are so vital nonetheless.

Sex is not everything to a man, certainly not enough to justify a long-lasting marriage or long-lasting love. It is not a foundation you marry for. But it is without doubt the number one thing which brings him instant happiness, sorry society but it is. If you sent a man a text saying *"when you get home darling would you like a nice shepherd's pie I have cooked or I could give you a blow job instead"*, well within 30 seconds of reading that, he is in the car, ordering Deliveroo for you both and rushing back to jump in the shower as quickly as he can.

91% of men in my survey said they would prefer a Blow Job over food and quite simply the other 9 percent were lying.

There are 15,000 sex workers on the website *adultwork* as I mentioned before. There aren't 15,000 lady chefs offering food for a man to choose from. A man does not cheat because someone cooks better than you do, but nonetheless that does raise an interesting thought.

If the way to a man's heart is through his stomach then if on his way home he popped into another lady's house and she gave him a lasagne with no sex, has he cheated or not?

I have looked online at the endless articles on how to save a marriage by endless experts but I'm afraid to say once again that they are obviously not men. They have been written in a way that society feels is right and what women I guess wants to be right and who can blame her. But they are simply telling you what you want to hear rather than confronting the brutal raw truth of man's search for *PANDER*. In the private survey I carried out, 66% of men said sex was the most important thing to them in a relationship and 84% said *LBJ* was the most important part of that.

To highlight this further, a typical article online written by a lady, in good faith I'm sure, described how to improve your marriage by suggesting these things

Show your good side

Change your appearance

Compromise

Take a break from each other once and a while

Find something in common

Not once do they mention *LBJ*. Why? Simply because it isn't politically to do so.

Ok, so how does a man actually like *LBJ* to be performed on him? God knows I didn't ask that question when I carried out my survey, it's a private thing and there are endless ways to do it. I will touch on it in a general sense though, I'm helpful like that.

However, what I'm now going to say about technique I understand totally could and would apply to man too in what he does for you, how he "performs", how he should try and give you what you want to enjoy sex.

But it's hard for me to comment on that, I can only tell it from a man's perspective.

Obviously for some men they won't know how they like it, if they have only had a few partners. But men do watch porn and they will see it there and be influenced by it. I know they don't get influenced by their friends because men never ever talk about it. It is unimageable a man describing to others how he prefers *LBJ* with his *balls being squeezed whilst a finger is slipped into his arse*.

But let's think about it seriously, if we can treat this subject seriously. Is the way you do a blowjob the same as when you started and therefore you just repeat that thing again and again?

Consider a Shepherd's Pie.

It was first developed as a meal in the early 1700's so 300 or so years ago. Whatever the original recipe was will have changed, roughly the same thing but 100's of variations. If you look at any of the celebrity chefs' books, Jamie Oliver, Gordon Ramsey, you will see a variation of it. The Ivy even have it on their menu which is totally different from any other.

So, with that in mind, why would you do *LBJ* the same way all the time? It's like the shepherd's pie, sometimes you go traditional, sometimes more exotic with some spice or twist. Depends on the mood.

Without laughing if you can, close your eyes now and think about the way you do it. This could be the single most important thing you can do for your partner to make him happy. And to date, how much times have you actually thought about that? I'm sure you will have had better things to do with your time with your kids running around your ankles and snotty noses to clear, but run with me. On many occasions, you will have thought about what to cook for the idiot man, what to wear on a night out to "impress" him, what you should get for his Xmas present, 100's of things but have you ever sat there and thought about the single most important thing in his shallow life?

And if I'm right on my theory, do the *LBJ* well and he will be a puppy dog in your hand and everything you want out of a relationship will follow. Isn't that worth thinking about?

It's all a bit weird though oral sex either way isn't it. No idea whoever thought of that as a good thing to do but it's not your obvious match up.

I mean think about the cleanliness issue. I'm guessing you spend forever being careful with germs in your everyday life yet you are now being asked to put his knob into your gob. He may have washed it 2 mins before, he may not have done, but if he did he certainly didn't with the bleach you put onto the kitchen side earlier that day because you are obsessed that a tiny bit of chicken left there could cross contaminate you. Yet mouth and cock have cross contamination written all over it in an unbelievable erotic orgy of germs.

I've even heard stories of escorts washing a man's knob before a blow job and I have to say technically they have a point. But not good for the old romance though is it. Say it's the first time you go down on him. The lighting is right, champagne on ice, candles everywhere, soft music on. Seductively you move down his body with your tongue on him, pausing only as you reach your desired target, driving him into a state of unimaginable sexual desire in the process. And as he closes his eyes waiting for your mouth to bring him to the greatest orgasm he has ever had, you whip out a pack of detox cleaning wipes, pull back his foreskin violently and wash his cock like it was the toilet seat after a dinner party.

I have no idea to be honest what is the best way to receive a blow job I'm sure it will vary man to man and as I said I have never had one discussion or heard one discussion on it over hundreds of thousands of chats in my life. But there are 32 variations of it apparently (google it) and so the greatest Xmas, birthday or valentines present you could ever give your man is to suggest to him one night you will perform as many of the 32 as you can and for him to give his top 5.

That could honestly be the greatest gift ever.

The standard version of *LBJ* is cock in mouth up and down for a couple of minutes, wank a bit, cum, over. Repeat in 7 days. But that's like getting him a normal coffee from Starbucks. Think about what else your man could have. How about he gets a medium latte with half low-fat milk, a dash of cinnamon and vanilla extract stirred 30 times and served with a cookie.

What I can also say on this subject is on the matter of where should the cum goes when mankind's orgasmic wonderland arrives as a result of your sterling efforts.

To be as clear and as blunt as I can be, apart from cumming inside you, the man you are with wants it in your mouth on your breasts or your face. Nowhere else. He is lying if he says he doesn't. If he says he prefers it that you look away as he is cumming, he is lying. There isn't one man on this earth who doesn't want it as I have described, if he had a choice. And when I mean not one man, I mean 100% of 6 billion people on this planet. If a man from the depths of Siberia suddenly pipes up now and says he doesn't, then he is lying too.

And how do I know that? Think logically. Will he really love it when the orgasm he has been saving up all week for is ruined, not only with the tension of having to tell you exactly when he is cumming so you can look away with pure disgust but also because if he does happen to time it wrong and it goes near your face, then he has to endure the sight of you running to the bathroom screaming with gagging sick noises before shoving two litres of Dettol, all over your face.

You won't find any porn film where that happens. And there is a reason for it.

Of course, in your relationship if your partner forces you to do something horrible or painful then that is simply not right. And that of course massively applies to sex and to this subject, if you don't like it don't do it of course that is the right decision. But on this particular topic, on this delicate but important subject, can I just offer up some tongue in cheek and playful advice to put things in prospective if you are wavering and have an open mind on the subject.

Run with me.

You would treat a bad cough with cough mixture which everyone hates. If you had to swallow it you would maybe take it 4 times a day, for 4 days so 16 times. That cures you of your cough and you are happy.

Swallowing his cum once a month is only 12 times a year. It's less awful therefore than cough mixture. And that is the intellectual rational of mankind.

The Blow Job Dark Arts

Finally, I am now going to suggest a way to use this new knowledge as the ultimate use of the dark arts, which is essentially the practice of getting that thing you wanted for free.

And this will work every single time. It goes like this

You are in the act of giving him *LBJ* and you wait for the right moment to pounce; timing is everything to maximise your advantage. Get him nicely worked up first.

Then you look at him with your seductive loving eyes

"*Enjoying it*" you purr

"*Oh, baby at this moment I would give you the world*" replies the dumb bloke as his balls are being lightly touched

Now at this point you can't let go of touching either his cock or his balls as you talk. You have to keep him on the edge still with the promise of the encore building. He wants that encore but that pause just means your opportunity has increased even more because he desperately needs you to carry on. At his moment you have a short-term power that he can never have over you, this is your defining moment, you hold every single card there is to hold in your relationship and it's time to play them.

"*Oh, honey*" you whisper like a Russian mistress "*you are just so lovely but you know the only think I want really is a Samsung RG23 fridge with ice dispenser in stainless steel* "

"*If I could get that for you right now baby I would*" the sucker replies

It's at this point that you have be prepared. The computer has to be ready somewhere with the page loaded and all things completed. You have to act now. If he cums you won't get it in the morning, even if he has promised it, he will just say

"*We have a perfectly good fridge Tina stop being so flippant about money and consider fiscal responsibility for once"*

So, without stopping touching him, lean over and say *"oh the computer is here, it would be such a turn on baby if you pressed buy for me"* as your tongue licks him some more

And he will press buy. And he will also get you extra ice cube trays, a 12 pack of diet coke and a 3-year warranty all at the same time.

Essentially the lesson here is this.

You are down there anyway, so why not make something out of the tight git.

Printed in Great Britain
by Amazon